**BETTER
SUNDAYS
BEGIN
ON
MONDAY**

BETTER
SUNDAYS
BEGIN
ON
MONDAY

David
W. Manner

BETTER
SUNDAYS
BEGIN
ON
MONDAY

SUNDAY
15

MONDAY
16

52 Exercises for Evaluating Weekly Worship

Abingdon Press™
Nashville

BETTER SUNDAYS BEGIN ON MONDAY:
52 EXERCISES FOR EVALUATING WEEKLY WORSHIP

Copyright ©2020 by Abingdon Press

Library of Congress Control Number: 2020937420

ISBN: 978-1-7910-0473-6

Scripture quotations are taken from the Common English Bible, copyright 2011. Used by permission. All rights reserved.

20 21 22 23 24 25 26 27 28 29—10 9 8 7 6 5 4 3 2 1
MANUFACTURED IN THE UNITED STATES OF AMERICA

Contents

Contents

Contents

Acknowledgments

Thank you to my wife, Karen, for always making me better in everything I do or even attempt. She is one of the most creative people I know and, consequently, regularly challenges me to think gray spiritually, emotionally, and intellectually. Thank you to my daughter, Jessa, for always being the life of any party and for surpassing our dreams about the joy of being a parent. Thank you to my son-in-law, Cullen, for making our daughter happy, completing our family, and loving her even more than we do, even though I didn't think that was possible.

I owe a debt of gratitude to my parents, Bill and Clare Manner, for their support and encouragement throughout my life and ministry. This book is just one of many examples of how their prayer support helps me finish well. Thank you for your legacy of exemplary spiritual and married lives. If I am half the person you have been and continue to be, then my life will have been a success.

I am grateful to the Creative Team at Western Hills Church, Topeka, Kansas. You guys model every week what healthy worship evaluation looks like in an atmosphere of brutal honesty rooted in profound trust. You remind me through your worship-planning and implementation that churches are better when they try to figure things out together.

Thank you to the churches, pastors, worship leaders, and convention staff of Kansas-Nebraska Convention of Southern Baptists for allowing me to try some of these principles out on you.

I am indebted to the Robert E. Webber Institute for Worship Studies and its faculty for expanding my limited understanding of worship renewal and helping me not to coast through ministry this last decade.

Lastly, I would like to express posthumous thanks to Dr. Paul B. Clark, Jr., who not only served as a colleague in convention work and as a doctoral cohort collaborator but also walked with me as a close personal friend and worship renewal practitioner for over three decades. I am a better minister and worshipper having known him.

Introduction

Some worship-planning teams have implemented an evaluative process after their worship services each week. They meet regularly to reflect on what did and didn't work. This after-service evaluation is a postmortem of what has already occurred. By definition, a postmortem occurs only after death or after the damage has already been done. Postmortem evaluators say, "We'll do it better next time."

What if, in addition to the worship service postmortems, those individuals or planning teams also implemented a process of worship service premortem evaluations? Premortem is the process of applying prospective hindsight before an event or project occurs. Prospective hindsight is considering what might occur by envisioning the future outcome or imagining results based on the information at hand. Premortem evaluators say, "Let's get it right this time."

Maybe it's possible through these collective pre- and post-evaluative processes to improve, strengthen, and renew our worship services as they are being birthed, rather than just having to autopsy them after their passing. It should be noted that last-minute worship-service planning makes premortems virtually impossible and often contributes to painful postmortems.

Breaking down game film is a discipline sports teams often incorporate after each game. They review and discuss game videos in order to identify mistakes, make adjustments, consider radical changes, and highlight successes. The ultimate goal of this type of analysis is to facilitate individual and team improvements that will positively affect subsequent games. The fundamental reason why a team needs adjustments is not always evident in the middle of the game. Breaking down or evaluating all of the important elements after a game gives coaches and players the opportunity to isolate and assess individual plays and players in a more relaxed setting, away from the time constraints and pressures of the game.

So why aren't individual pastors, worship leaders, and even worship-leading teams regularly incorporating similar evaluative practices? One of the primary reasons is that implementing an individual or collaborative process of analyzing worship services or planning for upcoming services requires a deep level of humility, trust, and shared accountability. It also requires selfless leaders who are willing to sacrifice their own ideas, preferences, and interests for the greater worshipping good of the congregation.

Collaborative observations and the wisdom with which to respond to those observations will always be strengthened when the ages, gifts, experiences, and perspectives of the collective group are diverse. Advantages to enlisting an internal evaluation team include: candid responses from individuals and groups who already understand the doctrines, philosophies, personnel, and policies of your congregation; evaluations are from trusted leaders who have a vested interest in the process and results; and a greater degree of accountability for implementing the evaluation results in a timely and benevolent fashion. If you see the value in developing an evaluative team, it should include pastors, musicians, technicians, artists, interior designers, builders, multiple generations, and multiple ethnicities. Every element of the worship service, including the sermon, must be fair game for this type of evaluation to be successful.

A balanced approach to worship evaluation can be summative in that a congregation can learn from its previous worship failures and successes. But it can also be formative since it occurs during the development and conceptual worship service stages.

Better Sundays Begin on Monday offers weekly stand-alone foundational worship considerations to help you—individually or as a team—ask worship questions evaluatively rather than defensively. The weekly evaluation considerations are not contingent on the size of your church or its staff, so, consequently, they will apply to single-staff or multiple-staff congregations of various sizes, generations, and cultures. In addition to the weekly evaluation considerations of each chapter, several situational questionnaires are provided in the appendixes to help you and your team begin to dig a little deeper each week.

The fifty-two weekly evaluation considerations intentionally place more focus on a biblical, theological, and historical baseline worship philosophy rather than just service mechanics. So they will help you or your team first determine *why* you worship before ever considering *how* you worship. Worship renewal must be determined first by standardizing worship principles before ever considering worship practices. The reality is that worship service evaluation is already occurring in the hallways, in parking lots, and at lunch tables after our services. Why wouldn't we want to preempt those conversations with an intentional evaluative process?

My prayer is that *Better Sundays Begin on Monday* will be the starting point to help you and a team you develop, no matter how large or small, discuss and evaluate your worship services each week, moving beyond style to deeper biblical and theological content. When an intentional and collaborative process of weekly worship evaluation is implemented, the reality is that you as leaders will no longer receive all of the credit for worship successes. But fortunately, you won't receive all of the credit for worship failures either.

How to Use This Book

Better Sundays Begin on Monday was written to help your worship-leading team, church staff, or other select groups evaluate your worship each week. Each stand-alone chapter and discussion questions offers a weekly or bi-weekly tool to help encourage worship renewal. The following steps will help your teams best utilize these resources:

1. Plan a weekly or bi-weekly worship evaluation session as part of your regular worship team rehearsals, church staff meetings, or select group meetings. These resources are just as accessible for individuals or smaller worship-leading teams and church staffs as they are for larger ones.

2. Ask participants to read one of the fifty-two chapters prior to each evaluation session so they are prepared to respond to several discussion questions provided for each chapter.

3. Reading and discussing each chapter together should help your teams answer the questions, "What did we hear, and what must we do?" In other words, how can we apply what we have read and discussed to encourage worship renewal for our team and church?

4. Additional resources to help your team go even deeper are also available as appendixes. Several questionnaires and other team resources are provided as internal and external evaluation tools to potentially expand your pool of respondents to your entire congregation or even guests from outside of your congregation.

Chapter One
Creating Worship Tourists

In *Teaching a Stone to Talk*, Annie Dillard wrote, "Why do we people in churches seem like cheerful, brainless tourists on a packaged tour of the Absolute? The tourists are having coffee and doughnuts on Deck C. Presumably someone is minding the ship, correcting the course, avoiding icebergs and shoals, fueling the engines, watching the radar screen and noting weather reports radioed from shore. *No one would dream of asking the tourists to do these things.*"[1]

If we never involve our congregants as more than casual bystanders while we read, speak, sing, play, pray, testify, lead, mediate, commune, baptize, confess, thank, petition, and exhort, then how can we expect them to transform from passive spectators to active participators? Aren't we really creating worship tourists who select their destination based solely on their impression of the platform tour guide and excursion offered rather than worship travelers on a continuous journey?

Tourists, on the one hand, sample other cultures as long as they aren't too different from their own. They expect others to adjust to them. Inconvenience for a tourist is always inconvenient because it discourages pleasure and preference. Tourists only scratch the surface and ask what, when, and how much. They only go where the map takes them, are there to experience the sites, aren't willing to stray away from their native language, and always ask, "What's in it for me?" Worship tourists are onlookers or observers, much like they would watch an event or game. They are audience members or spectators who might be a fan or foe depending on who is playing and what is being played. And they think they are in the game because they are in the stands.

1

Travelers, on the other hand, willingly immerse themselves in cultures even when they might be radically different from their own. They adjust instead of expecting others to adjust to them. Inconvenience for a traveler is never inconvenient because it encourages discovery. Travelers always dig deep and ask who and why. They go where the road takes them, are there to understand the sites, attempt to learn new languages, and always ask, "What's in it of me?" Travelers are involved in the game because they are contributing to it. They relate to what is going on because it is larger than them. As participants they are engaged and involved in the game because they are actually on the field and not in the stands.

Leaders facilitate participative worship not just by depending on their own strengths and abilities but also by investing in the strengths and abilities of other congregants who are willing to subordinate their individual interests to the corporate concerns of the entire congregation. The leader who promotes participative worship taps into the collective resources and talents of others by affirming their value to worship health.

Participative worship is intentionally collaborative and is not guarded, territorial, or defensive. It trusts the creative abilities and resources of the whole in the planning, preparation, and implementation. Consequently, participatory leaders are not threatened when someone else gets their way or gets the credit. Participatory worship is a culture, not a one-time event.

Will Willimon wrote, "Many of the Sunday orders of worship consist of the pastor speaking, the pastor praying, the pastor reading, and the choir singing, with little opportunity for the congregation to do anything but sit and listen. When the Sunday service is simply a time to sit quietly, hear some good music and a good sermon, sing a hymn and then go home to eat dinner, no wonder many of our people get confused into thinking that Christ only wants passive admirers rather than active followers."[2]

The ultimate destination for worship tourists and travelers may be exactly the same. But the connection for the tourist is usually shallow and fleeting. The connection for the traveler, however, is always deep and continuous. The worship tourist endures the journey in order to reach the destination, while the traveler values the journey as part of the destination.

TEAM DISCUSSION QUESTIONS

- How can we move our congregants from passive spectators to active participators?

- What are we presently doing that may be discouraging or encouraging participative worship?

- What are some of those worship leadership elements we should be asking congregants to do so our leaders aren't doing everything for them?

- How will we know if we are accomplishing our goal of more congregational worship participation?

Chapter Two
Farm Team

Congregations tend to plan and implement in the moment since Sunday comes every single week. So thinking about keeping younger players or finding future players, singers, or even a primary worship leader is rarely a consideration until a vacancy occurs.

"Player development" is what Major League Baseball calls the grooming of younger, less advanced players in their minor league system. The so-called farm teams provide mentoring, training, coaching, and practical experience for younger players with the expectation that as a player matures, he will advance to a higher level of play and responsibility. The genius of the farm system is that players get better by playing regularly in smaller venues instead of just waiting for an opening to play in the major leagues. Teams are intentionally investing in younger players for the future. A major-league team with a weak farm system may have success for a time but will rarely carry that success into the future.

The value of worship player development is realized when a congregation attempts to fill a vacancy in their worship-leading team. What most find is that the pool of potential replacements *out there* is often very shallow. Those who are available are sometimes unknown and don't always resonate with the culture of the searching congregation. Implementing a farm-team model of grooming or developing younger, less advanced players from *in here* can offer a trusted and familiar resource pool for future players, singers, or primary leaders. Investing in those who already understand the culture, personality, worship language, and mission of your church has a far greater potential for future success.

I was challenged a number of years ago while attending a worship leadership conference to make a list of individuals who had intentionally taken the time to encourage and coach me in my early ministry years. The clinician gave us time to complete our list and then asked, "Have you told those individuals on your list how much you value that investment?" After returning home from the conference I drafted half a dozen thank-you notes to send to those mentors I had listed. Paul Williams was on that list.

Nearly four decades ago, I began my first full-time ministry position. Paul Williams served as a music and worship pastor in another church in our city. In my first week or two of ministry, he stopped by my office and didn't ask but told me he was going to pick me up the following Saturday to attend a music workshop with him. This wizened sage of music and worship ministry (he was probably forty years old) invested in a twenty-four-year-old worship-leading beginner not for what he could get from me but for what he could offer to and invest in me.

This first ministry position was one of those learning experiences that many of us have endured. Paul knew the history of our congregation and the challenges I would face way before I figured it out. He never offered useless advice or platitudes when I was struggling to stay or questioning whether I missed God's calling. He just became a friend who graciously listened, encouraged, and was available every time I needed his wisdom.

Before Paul died in 2010 from complications of Acute Myelocytic Leukemia, he had served first as music and worship pastor for thirty-five years and then, beginning in 1992, as a full-time lyricist, clinician, and composer. Even though I moved to a different state, Paul continued to coach and mentor me by sending packets of his new music every few months with a humorous personal note of encouragement and a loving note to my family. I'm sure others received similar packets and notes from Paul. My relationship with him was not unique, but he had the ability to make each person feel as if it were. I'm not certain I'd still be in ministry now if Paul Williams hadn't taken the time to help shape and develop me as a younger leader then.

Our success in worship ministry will be judged not just on how well we did it ourselves each Sunday, but on how well we helped train others to do it too. If churches want great worship leaders in the future, they must invest in not-yet-great worship leaders in the present. Imagine, then, one of those congregations so effectively implementing this player-development model that they are able to groom more worship leaders than they actually have places for them to serve. Then imagine the kingdom value of that congregation getting to farm out those trained leaders to other congregations who were not as prepared to fill their own vacancies.

TEAM DISCUSSION QUESTIONS

- What system do we presently have in place to secure players, singers, and tech substitutes when team members are absent?

- How are we encouraging younger artists to develop their skills for potential worship leadership in the future?

- Within the limitations of our budget, leadership, and facilities, how can we implement a formal or informal training process for younger worship leaders?

- What opportunities do we have or can we create for younger leaders to use their gifts publicly before they are ready to lead in the primary worship services?

Chapter Three
Childish Worship-Leading

The character traits most of us learned as children are sometimes forgotten in our worship-leading relationships at church. Life skills such as sharing, cooperation, conflict resolution, respecting others, being willing to compromise, kindness, empathy, and humility can be set aside to guard our territory in the name of artistic excellence. So instead of adjusting our actions according to the collective needs of our worship-leading teams, we sometimes revert to selfish tactics to get our own way without considering the cost. Communal relationships that should be modeling "we're all in this together" can sometimes mean "we're all in this together just as long as I am in it just a little bit more."

Worship-leading teams that are intentionally collaborative, by contrast, are not guarded, territorial, defensive, or competitive. They are not threatened when someone else gets their way or gets the solo. They model sacrifice and humility. The default of a collaborative worship-leading team is always trust in the combined input of the whole.

When the disciples asked Jesus who the greatest was in the kingdom of heaven, he responded by calling for a little child and asking him to stand among them. Then he said, "Those who humble themselves like this little child will be the greatest in the kingdom of heaven" (Matt 18:1-4). Humility is one of the most difficult qualities for worship leaders to embrace and sustain. It's always a challenge to be both up front and unassuming.

Character is the outward manifestation of our inward nature and qualities. Our character is framed by our moral integrity, ethical standards, and spiritual foundational principles. It is not innate so it must be learned and practiced regularly or it is easily forgotten or ignored. Our character lets others know who we really are even when our situations are difficult or when conflicts

7

arise. Worship teams could learn or relearn some of those character traits that seem to flow so freely and unashamedly from children.

WONDER

Worship-leading should cause us to be curious, fascinated, surprised, and captivated. Children radiate these characteristics, but as adults we seldom do. We have replaced worship wonder with worship that is controlled and scripted. When we lose our wonder we are rarely wowed, amazed, or awed as we lead. If we are never surprised by the Holy Spirit, then how can we expect our congregants to be filled with awe and say, "We have seen remarkable things today" (Luke 5:26).

COOPERATION

Children learn early that always expecting to get your way, being a bully, not resolving conflict with kind words, not considering the needs of others, and not seeing things from another's point of view are not an option. When worship-leading teams model teamwork in rehearsals and from the platform, then their attitudes of cooperation will be contagious to the congregation they are trying to lead. Cooperation means we are willing to regulate our own feelings and impulses and consider the feelings and impulses of others for the good of the team. Cooperation reminds us that our worshipping "body isn't one part but many" (1 Cor 12:14).

TOLERANCE

Children seem to have a higher capacity to accept differences in others than we do. They learn intolerance from us. Worship leadership intolerance can be manifested musically and stylistically, as well as relationally and culturally. Leading worship with tolerance doesn't mean we are willing to compromise musically or theologically with our team members, but it might require us to be more tolerant systematically and stylistically with them.

RESILIENCE

Resilience is the elasticity that seems to allow children to recover quickly from radical change. It's the willingness to give things a try with an attitude of flexibility for the good of the whole. Leading worship with resilience averts relational catastrophes by creating a culture of pliability and forgiveness when mistakes are made. Worship-leading often requires us to adjust in the moment. Resilience allows us to make those adjustments by keeping our focus on "things above and not things on earth" (Col 3:2).

As worship leaders there are times when we need to be reminded what we once learned as children. When we remember it will give new meaning to the Scripture passage, "Train children in the way they should go; when they grow old, they won't depart from it" (Prov 22:6).

TEAM DISCUSSION QUESTIONS

- What guidelines can we put into place to make sure humility is a foundational characteristic for all of our worship leaders?

- How can we plan and lead well-ordered worship services while still leaving room for the Holy Spirit to surprise us?

- How will we initiate corrective measures with team members if character issues arise?

- In what ways can we practice these childish characteristics without compromising our desire for excellence?

Chapter Four
Tall Poppy

No matter how large or small, every church should be developing distinctly and becoming uniquely the congregation God has called them to be. Loving the Lord with heart, soul, mind, and strength and loving our neighbor as we love ourselves are never contingent on congregational size or abilities. It is instead our offering of all we have at that time and all we are in that moment.[1]

"Tall poppies" are persons whose accomplishments seem to elevate them above their peers. And "tall poppy syndrome" describes the resentment, jealousy, and envy that those peers have. Instead of improving themselves, peers will level the playing field by trying to bring down a "tall poppy" to their level. The tall poppy is criticized, attacked, and cut down to size.[2]

The potential for worship-leading envy is high since we don't have to look very far to find another church with younger leaders, unlimited players, more celebrity, and an edgier band or larger choir that sings with more passion and has a better platform presence. Worship-leading envy is irrational and covetous discontent as the result of another's perceived superior qualities, advantages, achievements, and successes.

Sometimes instead of trying to improve our own worship-leading skills or being willing to champion the worship-leading successes of our colleagues in other churches, we assume and even publicly claim that the success of others must only have been possible through stylistic superficiality, musical adulteration, or theological compromise.

The worship in our churches will never measure up because of what we are often trying every Sunday to measure up to. To measure up means to be as good as, to have the same qualifications as, to reach a certain standard as, to be of high enough quality for, or to compare with something or someone else. Trying to measure up to the worship of another congregation can be like running on a treadmill. As long as we keep our eyes focused ahead, we can log miles safely. But when we look to the left or right, our feet follow our eyes and cause us to veer off course or even wipe out. The writer of Hebrews said it this way: let's "run the race that is laid out in front of us . . . and fix our eyes on Jesus, faith's pioneer and perfecter" (Heb 12:1-2).

Comparing our worship to the worship of another congregation means we are trying to measure up to a standard God has called them to, not the one God has called us to. And God obviously sees the value of our calling even in those seasons when we don't. Keeping our eyes on Jesus instead of others means we lead worship with contentment, not comparison. It's a discipline that is not always fun and even seems painful at the time. Later, however, it yields the peaceful fruit of righteousness for those of us trained by it (Heb 12:11).

As worship leaders, we could learn a lot from MacGyver, the main character in an action-adventure television series that ran for several seasons in the 1980s. The show followed secret agent Angus MacGyver as he solved complex situations with everyday materials. Using common items on hand, MacGyver was able to find clever and often unbelievable solutions for seemingly unsolvable problems.

Offering what we have is not settling for mediocrity, nor is it a license for laziness. We still need to pray that God would send more people, stronger leaders, stellar players, and greater opportunities to influence our community and the world. But like MacGyver, we can't wait until all of the people and pieces are in place to begin. Instead, we have to create something unbelievable with what God has made available.

TEAM DISCUSSION QUESTIONS

- How can we learn from other congregations without just imitating what they are doing?

- What worship practices have we recently implemented that are unique to our congregation?

- What guardrails should we put in place to ensure our desire to get better and grow bigger doesn't cause jealous comparisons with other congregations?

Chapter Five
Sense of a Goose

It's difficult for the worship of your church to be healthy if the relationships of its platform leaders aren't. Healthy worship teams embrace a unified goal of helping each other help others to worship. Unhealthy worship teams function as independent contractors who play and perform dependent on their own talent alone. Even if those team members are producing individually, you'll never experience extraordinary worship leadership until you agree you're all in this together.

Every fall most of us observe flocks of geese flying to the southern part of the United States to escape the bitter cold of winter. Worship teams could better learn how to work together by observing the *V*-formation flight of these geese.

SIGNS YOUR WORSHIP TEAM HAS THE SENSE OF A GOOSE

- *You share leadership with each other.*

    The goose flying in front of the *V*-formation expends the most energy since it's the first to break the flow of air that provides lift for the geese that follow. When the lead goose tires, it moves to the rear of the formation where the resistance is lightest. This rotation happens perpetually throughout their journey. Consequently, each member of the flock serves as a leader as well as a follower.

    Worship teams that share leadership are not competitive. They consider and leverage the creative abilities and resources of all in the planning, preparation, and implementation. They are not threatened when someone else gets their way or gets the credit. They understand sacrifice and humility.

12

- ### *You draft for each other.*

Much like cyclists in a road race, when the geese fly in formation they draft for the bird immediately following. The entire flock then achieves a much greater flying range than if each goose flew on its own. As a result, they arrive at the destination quicker because they are lifted up by their combined energy and enthusiasm.

The United States sends a team of runners who are blind to compete in the Summer Paralympic Games every four years. These world-class athletes are paired with sighted guides to run with them. They are connected at the wrist by a small piece of rope called a tether to help them stay in their lane. The guides look ahead to call out potential obstacles and keep them informed of how far they have left to reach the finish line. The encouragement and protection the guide offers allow the runners who are blind to compete at a much higher level. What a great worship team model of drafting for others when some might be discouraged or standing in the gap when others are weary.

- ### *You cheer for each other.*

Geese frequently honk as they fly in formation. Scientists speculate this honking is a way to communicate and cheer for each other. Those repeated honks announce all is well and are encouragement to those out front to stay at it and keep on keeping on.

When training for a distance run, novice and even more advanced runners often find training encouragement by running with others. Running partners can offer motivation or challenge for each other to increase or decrease their pace. It's much easier to go farther when you aren't doing it alone. Once the training is complete and those runners are competing in a distance race, there are crowds that line the streets to cheer for them. Your worship team can serve as a great cloud of witnesses who surround and cheer for each other. Many of those encouragers have already gone before us paving the way and modeling what endurance looks like. Paul reminded the church at Philippi that watching out for what is better for others is better than watching out for our own good (Phil 2:4).

- ### *You protect each other.*

Scientists have discovered that when a goose becomes ill or is injured and has to drop out of the formation, two other geese will also fall out of formation to stay with the weakened goose. The other geese stay with that injured goose to protect it from predators until it is either able to fly again or dies. Wounded leaders might be overcome when trying to heal alone. So whether your team is rotating, flapping, honking, or helping, the combined efforts will better enable you to accomplish together what you are unable to do alone.

TEAM DISCUSSION QUESTIONS

- How can we preventively assess the spiritual, emotional, and physical health of our worship leaders to help avert a crisis?

- Is our worship leadership structure causing a culture of competitiveness or helping us avoid it?

- In what ways can we encourage each other to run the race with endurance?

- Do we have a process for worship team members to disengage for a season for health reasons and then reconnect when they are healthy again?

Tree of 40 Fruit

Being unified is the state of being united, linked, or joined together as one in spite of diversities and differences. Uniformity, however, is the state or quality of being the same. A healthy worshipping congregation and the worship team that leads it require unity but not necessarily uniformity.

A tuning fork is a *u*-shaped acoustic resonator made from an elastic metal. Its tines vibrate at a constant pitch by striking them against a hard surface. Once struck, a tuning fork emits a pure musical tone that is used as a standard to tune a variety of instruments.

A standard is the basis or model to which something else should be compared. It is determined by those in authority as a rule for measuring the quality or value of something.

A. W. Tozer wrote, "Has it ever occurred to you that one hundred pianos all tuned to the same fork are automatically tuned to each other? They are of one accord by being tuned, not to each other, but to another standard to which each one must individually bow."[1] What is the standard to which your worship is tuned?

Your worship is out of tune...

- if what's in it for me is your standard.

- if coat and tie or untucked shirt and jeans is your standard.

- if hymns or modern worship songs are your standard.

- if the styles and practices of another congregation or artist are your standard.

15

- if musical excellence alone is your standard.

- if worship band, orchestra, choir, or worship team is your standard.

- if when and where you worship is your standard.

- if fixed or free liturgy is your standard.

- if the creativity of novelty or the comfort of nostalgia is your standard.

But if your standard is instead who, why, and in what power we worship—the Father, Son, and Holy Spirit—then your worship will always be perfectly tuned.[2] According to Paul, being unified is living "together in a manner worthy of Christ's gospel" (Phil 1:27). We can exercise a variety of different worship gifts, callings, and styles and still be unified as long as our root solidarity is not our worship expressions but the gospel.

Art professor Sam Van Aken combined art and farming to develop an incredible Tree of 40 Fruit. He bought an orchard that was about to be shut down and spent several years chip grafting a variety of trees onto a single fruit tree. In the spring, Van Aken's tree is a stunning patchwork of multicolored blossoms, producing fruit such as plums, peaches, apricots, nectarines, cherries, and almonds. The roots of each of these trees are united even though the fruit or outward expressions are diverse. Each tree offers just the right amount of each of forty varieties.[3]

The Apostle Paul said it this way to the church at Corinth, "Christ is just like the human body—a body is a unit and has many parts; and all the parts of the body are one body, even though there are many" (1 Cor 12:12). "Certainly the body isn't one part but many. If the foot says, 'I'm not part of the body because I'm not a hand,' does that mean it's not part of the body? If the ear says, 'I'm not part of the body because I'm not an eye,' does that mean it's not part of the body? If the whole body were an eye, what would happen to the hearing? And if the whole body were an ear, what would happen to the sense of smell? But as it is, God has placed each one of the parts in the body just like God wanted. If all were one and the same body part, what would happen to the body? But as it is, there are many parts but one body" (1 Cor 12:14-20).

TEAM DISCUSSION QUESTIONS

- How do we champion a worship-leading culture of unity but not necessarily uniformity without compromising our mission?

- What opportunities are we affording artists to use their art in worship beyond our traditional offerings?

- What is the standard to which our worship is tuned?

- Can all of our worship team members verbalize our standard, and is it evident as they lead?

Chapter Seven
Dear Non-Singing Pastor

Pastor, we depend on you as a primary worship leader for our congregation. We do agree that your leadership centers more on worship through the Word and Table than through the music. We also understand and affirm that worship can't be contained in one expression such as music.

But when you choose not to sing, we wonder if you really view the musical worship elements as an appetizer before the main course or the warm-up band before the headliner. When you study sermon notes instead of singing, it gives the impression you are unprepared, reminiscent of a freshman cramming for a final exam. Pastor, we desire worship that is a continuous conversation with a variety of worship expressions instead of just stand-alone elements of music and preaching. We long for you to teach and model active and fully engaged participatory worship instead of passively giving permission to others not to sing too.

You may have read or heard stories of expeditions to the summit of Mount Everest, the highest peak in the world. If so, you'll recognize the names Sir Edmund Hillary or George Mallory. Because of their Everest ascents, these men were recorded as some of the greatest climbers in history. But the names of the Nepali guides who helped these great climbers achieve those records are probably unrecognizable to most of us outside the Everest climbing community. These often-unnamed men and others like them have in fact made the fastest and most ascents at the youngest ages.

Hundreds of climbers attempt to reach the summit of Everest every year with the help of guides from the Sherpa ethnic group who are from the mountains of Nepal. Sherpas prepare the route, fix the safety ropes, carry the supplies, set up the camps, and then help the climbers attempt to reach their goal of conquering Everest. Without the assistance of these Sherpas, most climbers would fail to reach the summit.

The Sherpas are so successful because they understand the mountain themselves before attempting to assist others. They are locals who know the mountain, know the culture, know the people, and consequently, know the potentials and limitations. The Sherpas are the most skilled mountain climbers in the world, but their names aren't often known because their job isn't about the celebrity of their own success; it is about helping others succeed.

As pastor, you have the sacrificial and not-always-noticed responsibility to help others with less skill, less training, and often less knowledge. Some of them will be experienced and some won't. And some will have been hurt in previous climbs and are trying to find the courage to climb again. Like that of Sherpas, your worship-leading success will not be evaluated just on how well you reached the summit yourself, but on how you assisted others to reach the summit too.

So with the humility of a Sherpa we ask you to help lead us to the summit. Join us in full-throated singing so that all of our voices, including yours, might unite in communal utterances of praise, thanksgiving, confession, dedication, commitment, lament, and response. When this occurs, our songs will communicate vertically and horizontally in a unified voice so compelling that it can't possibly be stopped (Ps 30:12).

TEAM DISCUSSION QUESTIONS

- How do we convey to our congregation and perhaps even to our pastor that we look to him or her as one of our primary worship leaders?

- What are the attitudes and actions that give evidence that our pastor is considered one of our primary worship leaders?

- How can our musicians and pastor work together to create worship flow as a continuous conversation instead of stand-alone elements of music and preaching?

Chapter Eight

Bandwagon Effect

My childhood home was a frame house located next door to a small strip mall. The attic of our home had been converted into a great bedroom for a young boy. That strip mall adjacent to our home consisted of a radio and television shop, various business offices, and a pharmacy at the far end of the mall. From my bedroom window I could see across the roofline of the five or six small stores and shops.

One night, my parents were awakened by the pharmacy's burglar alarm. My dad contacted the police and then awakened me to let me know what was happening. We watched in the darkness of my bedroom as a thief attempted to access the pharmacy through its roof with a pickaxe. When the police arrived, the burglar tried to elude them by running across the rooftops toward our house. It was obvious he intended to jump into the gap between the stores and our house to escape capture. But my always-prepared dad temporarily blinded the intruder by pointing a huge flashlight in his eyes the moment he jumped.

From the street it appeared that our house and the strip mall were only one-story structures. In reality, because of the slope of our side yard, where the thief intended to jump was actually three-stories high. The hapless criminal landed in a heap on our metal garbage cans and was easily apprehended and arrested by the police. He had jumped blindly without considering all of the circumstances or the consequences.

During the nineteenth century, an entertainer named Dan Rice traveled the country campaigning for President Zachary Taylor. Rice's bandwagon was the centerpiece of his campaign events, and he encouraged those in the crowd to "jump on the bandwagon" and support Taylor. The campaign was so successful that Taylor was elected president, prompting future politicians to employ bandwagons in their campaigns in hopes of similar results.[1]

The idiom "jumping on the bandwagon" suggests following the crowd for the excitement of the event rather than any firm conviction in its direction or truthfulness. In other words, jumping blindly without considering all of the circumstances or consequences. The bandwagon effect occurs when the application of beliefs, ideas, fads, or trends increases the more others have already adopted them. Churches even have the tendency to espouse certain behaviors, styles, or attitudes just because it seems like everyone else has. The implication being that since it is right for so many others, it must also be right for us.

Jumping on the bandwagon explains why there are fashion trends. During sports championships it is evident in the increase of fans. In health it shows up in the latest diet or fitness craze. In social media it is obvious in the number of app or platform downloads. In music it is measured by online rankings. And in worship it is usually apparent in the song set.

The theological implication of a church that jumps on the latest worship bandwagon is that it sometimes ignores or overrides its own beliefs, cultures, or contexts just because others are doing it. Instead of encouraging spirit and truth worshippers, it creates liturgical lemmings.

It is true that congregations often need to make and should be making regular worship adjustments, including the latest songs, styles, or technological tools. But instead of always being early adopters and jumping without considering circumstances and the potential consequences, those congregations should instead be discerning and determining their worship practices by praying together, reading Scripture together, coming to the Lord's Table together, mourning together, rejoicing together, sharing ministry together, playing together, and then finally singing their song sets together.

TEAM DISCUSSION QUESTIONS

- How do we determine when and how often to try new things in our worship context?

- What filters can we put in place to ensure we aren't just jumping on the latest worship trend?

- How can we determine if what is popular in other churches is appropriate for our church?

- Is there a way for our team to consider all the circumstances or potential consequences before we actually jump into something new?

Chapter Nine
Mindless Worshippers

If our church services convey that worship starts when we start it and ends when we end it, if all worship resources and energies are spent preparing for and presenting a single hour on Sunday, if we aren't exhorting our congregation and modeling for them how to worship not only when we gather but also when we disperse, then we are enabling mindless worshippers.

Jesus's greatest commandment was to love God with all our heart, being, *mind*, and strength and also to love our neighbor as ourselves (Mark 12:30-31). Paul's exhortation to the church at Philippi and us was that "if anything is excellent and if anything is admirable, focus your thoughts on these things: all that is true, all that is holy, all that is just, all that is pure, all that is lovely, and all that is worthy of praise. Practice these things: whatever you learned, received, heard, or saw in us" (Phil 4:8-9).

Worshipping with our minds allows us to approach worship with knowledge, insight, reason, memory, creativity, inquiry, imagination, and even doubt. If we offer our prayers superficially, if we read and listen to Scripture texts mechanically, if we gather at the Lord's Supper Table hastily, and if we only sing our songs emotionally, the end result is often mindless worship.

Congregants could learn a lot from the Jews who believe the Sabbath begins at sundown. Then the activities and things with which we fill our minds the night before could better frame our worship attitudes as we gather on the Sabbath. What we do, whom we spend our time with, what we watch, and what we think about could negatively or positively influence our worship attitudes as we gather.

My daughter was five years old the first time our family vacationed at Walt Disney World. After months of planning and days of travel, the final preparations for and anticipation of the first day at Magic Kingdom was almost too much excitement for her to contain.

Like a firefighter, she selected and laid out her clothes the night before so she could jump into them the next morning. Sleep eluded her with the anticipation of what was to come. She awakened early, quickly dressed, and inhaled breakfast so she would be ready to depart hours before the park even opened.

All conversation traveling from our resort to the park entrance centered on what she would observe, experience, eat, participate in, enjoy, and then take home at the end of the day. She had been thinking about it, dreaming of it, and planning, preparing, and longing for it. Her mind was so filled with it she couldn't contain the anticipation.

Empowering instead of enabling worshippers encourages them to think, plan, prepare, and dream about their worship actions autonomously. It gives them permission to take ownership in their own worship responses to God's revelation at the moment in which it occurs. Worship empowerment arises from the shallowness of dependency and leads to the full conscious, active, continuous, and thoughtful participation of each worshipper.

Worship or love of God and others must be something with which we fill our minds or it can become self-serving. Unless we are thinking about it, considering it, processing it, meditating on it, studying it, and learning how to get better at it, how will we teach others how to do it? Until we move beyond enabling our congregations to actually empowering them to think about their worship individually, we'll never encourage deep calling unto deep worship that also engages their minds (Ps 42:7).

TEAM DISCUSSION QUESTIONS

- What verbal instructions are we using that might imply our worship starts and stops with the opening and closing songs?

- In what ways can we encourage our congregants to prepare for gathered worship before they actually arrive?

- How can we empower rather than enable our worship participants?

- What kind of small-group training or sermon series could we initiate to encourage congregants to go deeper in their understanding of loving God with their minds?

Chapter Ten
Falling Up

Are participants in your worship services ever given an opportunity to express despair or grief as a corporate act of worship? Do they have the freedom to ask God *why* in your services through music, Scripture, prayer, and teaching? In light of the suffering of our culture, is an offering of praise enough, and can it stand alone at the expense of confession, mourning, contrition, penitence, and petition?[1]

Congregations are to be commended for their quick response to catastrophic events such as terrorist attacks, earthquakes, and hurricanes. Where we have fallen short is in the realization that individuals in our gathered worshipping congregation are also suffering through events that impact them just as catastrophically. Job loss, broken relationships with children, health concerns, and the deaths of loved ones are just a few of an almost endless list of laments. These laments that cause anxiety, anger, pain, and loneliness are impacting individuals just as radically as those tragic events that have impacted people around the world.

My wife and I had been married about five years when we began trying to start a family. We knew it wasn't unusual that we were unable to conceive in those first few months. But as those months stretched to years, we began to ask God why we, too, couldn't be parents. Most of our friends already had children. We went through the invasive and clinical processes of an infertility workup. Finally, after four years of testing and prodding we were able to conceive. We were elated but also cautiously optimistic since it had taken so long for us to get to this place. And since church people at that time didn't talk publicly about things like infertility, we decided to tell only our parents until we got beyond the first trimester. But in our physician visits prior to that marker, our doctor wasn't able to detect a heartbeat, indicating we would miscarry.

We were devastated and wondered if there might be a reason God didn't want us to be parents. Were we unworthy? Did God not trust us? Hadn't we been faithful in our service to him? Was there something we had or hadn't done to deserve this? Our questions and assertions were certainly not indicative of the character and presence of God so evident in other areas of our lives. But in that season it felt like we were walking through the darkness alone. How quickly we had forgotten that a Lord so intimately acquainted with his own grief was certainly big enough to handle ours. The sixteenth-century Spanish poet and Roman Catholic priest Saint John of the Cross referred to seasons such as this as "the dark night of the soul." Even Mother Teresa wrote, "I am told God lives in me—and yet the reality of darkness and coldness and emptiness is so great that nothing touches my soul."[2] The Sunday following our miscarriage I still had to lead worship even though I didn't feel like it. I didn't really believe those songs I was leading even though I had to lead them as if I did. That day I agreed with Jesus as he quoted the psalmist, "My God, I cry out during the day, but you don't answer; even at nighttime I don't stop" (Ps 22:2).

We have conditioned our congregations through happy songs, upbeat sermons, and platitudes to believe that a positive façade is somehow less threatening to God and our faith. Our public worship actions often convey to those struggling with sorrow, anger, anxiety, grief, or depression that all must be well with everyone here except me. Worship that never addresses those dark seasons is dishonest, as it publicly communicates two messages: either you must not feel *that* way or, if you feel *that* way, you must do something about it somewhere else—but not here.[3]

Authentic worship is the freedom without stigma to publicly admit that we can't handle the circumstances and struggles of life alone. Admitting to God and others that we can't do this on our own is in itself a profound act of worship. That worship language of lament is the healthy, open expression of pain, complaint, sorrow, anger, and frustration toward a God who understands what we are feeling. It is not the repression of praise but the divine process from which praise springs forth. It doesn't wallow in hopelessness but emerges from the paradoxical hope experienced through the expression of profound sorrow.

Lament allows a culture previously conditioned to avoid the public admission of anger, grief, or sorrow the permission to cry out to God without fear of reprisal. Michael Jinkins reminds us that "when we refuse to lament, we effectively deny the faithfulness of God and hide our naked lives from God's gaze amid the brush of the gardens in which we dwell, ill at ease, but unable to confess and be comforted."[4]

Worship is always easier when things are going our way, when we have a job, a healthy family, a lovely home, and financial security. But what about

25

when the daily events of life threaten to consume us? If worship is continuous, why wouldn't you also worship then?

Worship is our response to who God is, what God has done, and what God continues to do. God's revelation is perpetual, meaning it doesn't start and stop according to the various circumstances of life; therefore, our responses shouldn't either.

- Even when the Sunday hymns, songs, and sermons fall short when expressing how you really feel, why wouldn't you worship then?

- Even when it seems like everyone else is better off than you are, why wouldn't you worship then?

- Even when complaint or anger is the only response you can come up with, why wouldn't you worship then?

- Even when "how long?" is the only things you can ask, why wouldn't you worship then?

- Even when your family is incomplete because of infertility and miscarriage, why wouldn't you worship then?

- Even when job loss, a broken marriage, or health stress causes you to doubt God's provision, why wouldn't you worship then?

- Even when depression or anxiety overwhelms you, why wouldn't you worship then?

If our Sunday worship is to be truly authentic, it can't ignore the darkness occurring in the lives of those with whom we worship. If congregants are expected to walk through those dark seasons alone and outside of the gathered worshipping body, how can we expect them to walk with that gathered worshipping body once they reach the other side? Embracing that raw and transparent language of lament in our public worship will require profound trust. But when it occurs, our unified tears will enhance our vision. Those corporate tears will give us new eyes to discern the God who suffers with us. Those tears will offer comfort and bring us fresh understanding that God is nearby, sharing our humanity in all its bitterness and blessedness.[5]

TEAM DISCUSSION QUESTIONS

- How do we balance our song selections and verbal instructions so that our singing allows our congregation to express a variety of emotions?

- Without offering platitudes, how can we communicate to our congregation that our worship is a safe place for them to express pain?

- What obstacles might we face in our context if we decide to insert lament as a part of our worship language?

- How can we balance offering a variety of worship emotions in the limited service time we have each Sunday?

Chapter Eleven
Worship-Leading Pharisees

Scripture classifies the Pharisees as the strictest of all the Jewish religious sects. Unlike other groups during this time, they clung to their laws and traditions even at the expense of the joy of God's law. Jesus rebuked them numerous times for their hypocrisy, pretension, self-righteousness, and stiffness.

Fartlek is a running term of Swedish origin that literally means "speed play." Running fartleks involves varying your pace throughout your run by alternating between sprints and slow jogs. It becomes a game of experimenting with various paces, ultimately strengthening both speed and endurance. Running fartleks is a fun way to give new life to monotonous training runs as well as to rigorous speed intervals.

Leading worship is often serious but can also be enjoyable when we allow it to be. If the race we are running has become tedious and we are constantly berating our teams and congregants for not living up to our expectations, then maybe we need to lighten up and again experience the joy set before us. When was the last time you were joyous while leading worship? Maybe a more telling question is, "When was the last time those whom you lead were joyous because of your attitude as their leader?"

It's true that worship leaders carry a heavy load in the preparation and presentation of worship. We are usually the most talented musically and technologically in the room, and it's always a challenge to be both upfront and unassuming. But if in the name of excellence or musical purity we worship leaders start suggesting that what we lead and the style in which we lead it is the only tenable option, then we, too, need to lighten up lest we slide into worship-leading Pharisaism.

SIGNS YOU ARE A WORSHIP-LEADING PHARISEE

• *Worship service selections are determined by your favorite style instead of by biblical and theological content.*

"You ignore God's commandment while holding on to rules created by humans and handed down to you. Jesus continued, 'Clearly, you are experts at rejecting God's commandment in order to establish these rules.'" (Mark 7:8-9)

• *You disappear when it's time to set up or tear down.*

"For they tie together heavy packs that are impossible to carry. They put them on the shoulders of others, but are unwilling to lift a finger to move them." (Matt 23:4)

• *You lead songs about praise always being on our lips during the service and then berate the tech team after the service.*

"This people honors me with their lips, but their hearts are far away from me." (Matt 15:8)

• *Your audience is not an audience of one.*

"They believed, but they loved human praise more than God's glory." (John 12:43)

- *You accuse any ministry more successful than yours of being stylistically superficial, musically adulterated, or theologically shallow.*

  "All the crowds were amazed and said, 'This man couldn't be the Son of David, could he?' When the Pharisees heard, they said, 'This man throws out demons only by the authority of Beelzebul, the ruler of demons.'" (Matt 12:23-24)

- *You canonize or criticize either hymns or modern worship songs.*

  "But when the chief priests and legal experts saw the amazing things he was doing and the children shouting in the temple, 'Hosanna to the Son of David!' they were angry. They said to Jesus, 'Do you hear what these children are saying?'" (Matt 21:15-16)

- *You measure your level of artistry and spirituality against others.*

  "Look, your disciples are breaking the Sabbath law." (Matt 12:2)

- *You've made dressing up or dressing down a worship prerequisite.*

  "Everything they do, they do to be noticed by others. They make extra-wide prayer bands for their arms and long tassels for their clothes." (Matt 23:5)

- *You've created the false dichotomy that if your style is virtuous, then theirs can't be.*

  "God, I thank you that I'm not like everyone else—crooks, evildoers, adulterers —or even like this tax collector. I fast twice a week. I give a tenth of everything I receive." (Luke 18:11-12)

- *Your microphone must be a little hotter and your spotlight a little brighter than all others.*

"They love to sit in places of honor at banquets and in the synagogues. They love to be greeted with honor in the markets and to be addressed as 'Rabbi.'" (Matt 23:6-7)

TEAM DISCUSSION QUESTIONS

- How do we hold each other accountable to a culture of excellence without it deteriorating into pharisaical command and control?

- What safeguards should we put into place to protect each other from the inevitable stresses and short tempers of busy seasons?

- What would benevolent correction look like for a team member who seems to be sliding into Pharisaism?

Chapter Twelve
Please, Sir, I Want Some More

Could you imagine the outcry from pastors and parishioners if sermons were limited to once a quarter or only on special occasions? Even though we never hear such a suggestion for the *Verbal Word* of sermons, we hear it often for the *Visual Word* of Communion. The argument for the infrequency of Communion is so that it doesn't become too ritualistic or repetitious and therefore insignificant. But that is exactly what it has devolved into as we've continued to observe it as supplemental instead of foundational.

Charles Dickens told the story of an orphaned nine-year-old boy named Oliver Twist. Oliver and scores of other orphans toiled in a miserable workhouse. The boys worked long hours, subsisting on three paltry meals of gruel, which was a watery food substance of unknown character offering little nutritional value. On one occasion, the boys drew lots to determine who would represent them in asking for more food. Oliver was selected and timidly moved forward with his bowl in his hands to make the famous request, "Please, sir, I want some more." One of his caretakers shrieked, "What? More?" And Oliver was chased around the dining hall tables by a band of well-fed caretakers.

Our understanding of Communion's symbolism has degenerated into a substance of unknown character offering little nutritional value. We know we have a spiritual mandate to observe this ordinance, yet we often wonder, "Is this all there is?" Can we ask for more within the parameters of our doctrine, denomination, embedded theological understanding, and history without fear of being chased around the Table by a band of well-fed doctrinal caretakers? For many congregations, observing Communion has become so routine that it no longer calls forth the reality it symbolizes. There is a need to discover it again with such freshness that it would be like experiencing it for the first time.[1]

When our daughter left for college a number of years ago, my wife and I were in a new season of remembrance. We missed having opportunities to spend time with her while she was away from home. In an effort to remember time spent with her, I regularly stepped into her bedroom just for a few moments. Spending time in the midst of a couple of decades of mementos and photographs scattered around her room allowed me to enter again into the remembrance and symbols of her life. Sometimes those remembrances caused me to grieve and weep for what would no longer be. Other remembrances caused me to laugh out loud. By returning often I discovered that the remembrance was rarely manifested in the same way twice. That is why I returned often.

We must stop being so afraid of making too much of the Table that we keep making too little of it. Wanting more will require worshippers to transform from the casual practice of just observing Communion to actually *entering in and living in the remembrance of it*. Living in that remembrance doesn't change the physical characteristics of the elements; it changes us. Living in the remembrance allows us not only to recall Jesus's death, burial, and resurrection but also to remember how those events impacted and continually impact our lives. When we live in the remembrance we are reminded that the story is not just Jesus's story but also our story as we are invited to step into Jesus's story. And living in the remembrance also reminds us that the final chapter is yet to come and we get to be a part of the unfolding of that story as insiders, not just as casual observers.

Repeating Communion frequently doesn't minimize its value; it enhances it. Repetition allows us to go this time where we might not have had the resolve to go last time. Once we grasp the magnitude of living in the remembrance of the Table, we will never again have to ask, "Is this all there is?" In fact, we may actually receive "far beyond all that we could ask or imagine by his power at work within us" (Eph 3:20). That is why we must return often to ask for more.[2]

TEAM DISCUSSION QUESTIONS

- Considering the culture of our congregation, how often is too often to celebrate Communion?

- Who determines the frequency of Communion in our church, and what are those deciding factors?

- Are there ways we can come to the Table more often without it becoming too routine or repetitious?

- How can we ask for more from the Table without compromising doctrinally?

Chapter Thirteen
Remember

Many of us just completed another designated Sabbath, or day of rest, which included numerous worship services, meetings, leadership responsibilities, and rehearsals—only to be reminded on Monday morning that Sunday comes again this week. Spiritual, emotional, mental, and physical resources are again completely depleted. Someone once said that leading worship is like having a baby on Sunday only to realize you are pregnant again Monday morning.

If your worship-leading schedule constantly feels like being caught in the force of a riptide that pulls you away from the safety of the shore; if the swift current regularly drags you under, rolls you on the sandy bottom, scratches up your elbows and knees, and fills your swim trunks with sand; if it seems to take longer each time for the current to lose its strength, release you, and allow you to swim to shore, then you'd better look for restful waters to restore your soul before you no longer have the resolve to kick to the surface and gasp for air (Ps 23:2).

Leading worship every Sunday can sanctify busyness rather than free us from it. Our church culture often values motion as a sign of significance, believing our efforts are essential to God's success in God's mission to the world. The stress of preparing multiple services each week and the demands of congregants, teams, and staff constantly vying for our time and attention may be exhausting our reserves. If this is true for you and your team, how can you expect to lead others to a place you no longer have the strength to go yourselves?

In his book *Leading on Empty*, Wayne Cordeiro uses surfing to illustrate how ministry longevity is possible. He writes, "Veteran surfers possess an uncanny sense of the ocean's currents and how waves behave. Their intuition tells them which ones to catch and which ones to let pass. They seem to discern which waves will carry them in and which waves will do them in! But one of the true marks of a veteran is not how he catches a wave, but whether he knows when and how to get off the wave."[1]

- When worship ministry feels like being caught in that riptide, remember that God reaches down from on high, grabs you, and takes you out of that water (Ps 18:16).

- When you worry if your children will even like church when they are no longer required to attend, remember that Jesus loves your children, too, and wants them to inherit God's kingdom (Luke 18:15-17).

- When your worship leadership shelf life seems to be moving quickly toward the expiration date, remember to run this ministry endurance race by keeping your eyes on Jesus (Heb 12:1-2).

- When congregants target your family because they are upset with you, remember God is your refuge and strength in times of great trouble (Ps 46:1).

- When you are tempted to quit every Monday morning, remember to be strong and don't lose heart, because your work will be rewarded (2 Chr 15:7).

- When you have to schedule your family vacation after the youth mission trip, children's camp, and vacation Bible school, but before the fall kickoff, remember to learn from Jesus's example of rest by putting on his yoke, not your own (Matt 11:28-30).

- When the senior adult potluck dinner is the only date night with your spouse, remember that New Testament church leaders were required to first demonstrate faithfulness at home before being considered for ministry (1 Tim 3:1-13).

- When you are the latest forced termination victim, remember to be brave and strong since God is with you wherever you go (Josh 1:9).

- When it seems like no one is holding your rope, standing in the gap, or watching your back, remember you have a great cloud of witnesses surrounding you (Heb 12:1).

- When you are always the first one to arrive and last one to leave, remember you are doing it in his power, not your own (Isa 40:29).

- When your creativity has been exhausted and burnout is causing you to coast, remember that the Lord is the potter and you are the clay, so it's the work of his hands, not yours (Isa 64:8).

- When you are attacked for initiating much-needed change, remember the Lord hates those who cause conflict in the community (Prov 6:16-19).

- When you don't have the resolve to take care of yourself spiritually, physically, and emotionally, remember the Lord gives you power when you're tired, revives you when you're exhausted, and increases your drive when reserves are depleted (Isa 40:29-31).

Remember, we should throw off any extra baggage and the sin that usually trips us. We can run with endurance this race that is laid out in front of us by focusing on Jesus. He endured for the sake of the joy out in front of him and modeled what it means not to grow weary and lose heart (Heb 12:1-3).

TEAM DISCUSSION QUESTIONS

- Are we as leaders modeling a healthy balance of ministry responsibilities, or are we sanctifying busyness?

- How can we make sure our worship team members aren't sacrificing their families because they are too busy with ministry responsibilities?

- How can we know if a team member might be close to burnout and need a break?

- What spiritual practices are we exercising together so that we aren't trying to do this on our own and are fixing our eyes on Jesus?

Chapter Fourteen
Cause and Effect

Worship doesn't invite God's presence; it acknowledges it. God has *called* us out of darkness into God's amazing light that we may speak of God's wonderful acts (1 Pet 2:9). The Father is *looking* for those who worship him in spirit and truth (John 4:23). God initiates, and we respond.

Cause and effect is a relationship in which a person, action, or thing makes another event, action, or thing occur. A cause must always precede an effect in order for that effect to occur. So the effect is then a consequence of the cause. A model for this cause-and-effect worship understanding is found in Isaiah 6:1-8. The holiness of God is revealed to the prophet Isaiah (cause), and his natural worship response is contrition (effect): "Mourn for me; I'm ruined!" (Isa 6:5). God revealed God's mercy (cause), and Isaiah's worship response is service (effect): "I'm here; send me" (Isa 6:8). If our worship responses are the effect, then it is not possible for those worship actions to also be the cause.

What we sing or how we sing it can't cause a response because it is the response. God's revelation can't be generated by the effect since the effect is a response to the cause. As good as our various worship actions are, they still can't cause worship to occur, because those worship actions are the effect. Our worship actions may prompt, remind, exhort, prod, or encourage more effect, but they can't cause cause. We can celebrate the cause, but we can't create it. God causes, and we effect.

Worship is our response to the overtures of love from the heart of the Father. It is kindled within us only when the spirit of God touches our human spirit. Forms and rituals do not produce (cause) worship, nor does the disuse of forms and rituals. We can use all the right methods (effect), we can have the best possible liturgy (effect), but we have not worshipped the Lord until his Spirit (cause) touches our spirit.[1] It is true that we occasionally *bump into* God in our worship efforts.[2] When this occurs we usually assume the encounter was based on what we sang, said, or did and how we sang, said, or did it. We often take credit for instigating God's presence and try to replicate it in future services.

When I was a child my family traveled each summer from Oklahoma to Tennessee for a couple of weeks of vacation with grandparents. The twelve-hundred-mile round trip on those two-lane roads in a 1960 white station wagon seemed to take forever. The length of the trip was minimized through the anticipation and excitement that grandparents, aunts, uncles, and cousins were waiting expectantly for our arrival. As we turned down the farm road and my grandparents' house came into view, we could always count on seeing my grandmother sitting in the porch swing waiting and watching for us to arrive. She wasn't certain when we would get there, so she would have been waiting there for hours, looking for us and longing for our arrival.

Our worship doesn't initiate this worship conversation with God; he does. He is calling us out of darkness and looking for us to worship him in spirit and truth. He is present long before we arrive and is waiting patiently for us to acknowledge his invitation to respond to him and join his conversation.

TEAM DISCUSSION QUESTIONS

- How do we teach our congregation that worship is our response to what Christ does in us, not what our songs do to us?

- Are there certain words or phrases we need to remove from our worship vocabulary that might be suggesting our songs cause worship?

- How can we help our congregation better recognize and respond to God's revelation in their lives?

- Is it possible to teach this cause-and-effect concept during the worship services, or would it require a different forum?

Chapter Fifteen
Intergenerational Killer

How can congregations expect to have healthy intergenerational worship when they segregate by age in all of their other ministries during the week? The only time various generations connect is during an hour on Sunday around songs one generation or the other doesn't particularly like. If congregations are depending on the music of that one hour to be the solitary driver of intergenerational worship, then music can't help but get the solitary blame when conflict arises.

What if, instead, all generations attempted to connect by first learning to love, respect, and defer to one another outside of the worship service? Couldn't those relationships that develop outside of the services then positively affect the relationships inside the worship services as well?

Intergenerational worship is only possible if our common ground is *deference* instead of *preference*. Deference is a learned and practiced submission based on conviction; preference is based on feeling and traditionalism. Deference encourages worshippers to respond in spite of the traditionalism and embedded theology that previously influenced their thinking and actions. The willingness to defer to others offers a common ground that style and musical preferences never will.

Deference is the agreement that although we may not always love the music of our children and grandchildren, we are willing to sacrifice because we love our children and grandchildren. Deferring is setting aside our preferences for the good of and future of those children and grandchildren. It is possible for grandparents and grandchildren to worship together as long as the battle lines are drawn over who can offer or give the most instead of who deserves or demands the most. Healthy intergenerational worship may not

40

occur until worship leaders are willing to lead dispersed intergenerational worship before attempting to lead gathered intergenerational worship.

Here are six suggestions:

1. Lead different generations to pray for and with one another. Praying for and with one another is not just praying for another generation to change its mind. Praying for and with one another requires communication, vulnerability, honesty, trust, brokenness, and selflessness.

2. Lead them to read Scripture to and with one another. Scripture must be the foundation of intergenerational worship. Nothing softens the heart of a grandparent more than to hear his or her grandchild read the word of God.

3. Lead them to share ministry together. Shared ministry requires sacrifice, humility, and an investment of time and trust. Serving others together encourages and generates unity that our music sometimes can't.

4. Lead them to play together. Those relationships exemplified by the Acts 2 church of spending time together, having everything in common, breaking bread in their homes, and eating together with glad and sincere hearts are often foreign relationships beyond our own generation.

5. Lead them to the Table together. We keep trying to manufacture unity that is already available at the Communion Table. Unity is waiting for all generations there.

6. Lead them to sing together. If unity is the basis of intergenerational worship during the week, then unity will yield intergenerational worship on Sunday. When that occurs, how can we keep from singin our various songs together?

TEAM DISCUSSION QUESTIONS

- How can our worship team coordinate with the other ministries of the church to encourage intergenerational relationships?

- If our platform doesn't represent the generational dynamics of our church, then how can we begin moving toward resolving that inconsistency?

- In what ways can we help our congregants love those with whom they worship more than how they worship?

- How can we encourage equal sacrifice for all generations and a willingness to focus on deference instead of preference?

Chapter Sixteen
Loss Leader Easter

We've all seen the social media hyperlinks that entice readers to click on an advertisement or website by using a sensational or alluring headline. Clickbait exploits curiosity by providing just enough information to pique the interest of the reader. The main purpose of clickbait is to attract attention, sometimes even at the expense of quality or honesty. The intent is that once visitors click on a particular site, they'll see or experience something that causes them to stay and buy what you are promoting or selling.

Churches all over the world formulate plans for persuasive Easter worship services knowing they will potentially reach more attendees on that Sunday than on any other Sunday of the year. In an effort to entice more participation, some of those congregations plan gimmicks or hooks to get new guests in for the most meaningful day of the church year.

A *loss leader* is when a retail chain or business offers goods or services at a discount or below cost in order to draw consumers in. The strategy is that drawing them in will hopefully then *lead* them to buy additional items at a higher cost. So when those first-time guests attend and realize that worship actually requires presenting their bodies as a living sacrifice, what methods will congregations then need to employ to keep them (Rom 12:1)? In that context, "you get what you pay for" actually means that whatever you reach people *with* is what you will reach them *to*.

If churches really affirm Easter as the most important celebration of the year and the foundation of our hope for the future, then why do they limit its observance to a single Sunday? Remembering the Resurrection only on Easter is like remembering your marriage only on your anniversary.

Easter in the early church was much more than a one-day event. They not only remembered and celebrated that Christ died and rose again but also remembered and celebrated that he appeared following his resurrection, that he ascended, that the Holy Spirit descended, and that Jesus promised to return again.

In their great joy the early church began celebrating with Easter and continued for fifty days. Seven weeks of remembering would allow our churches to go much deeper into the Resurrection, Ascension, and Pentecost instead of trying to cram it all into one Sunday so we can move on to the next sermon series. Limiting it to a single day can give the impression that its observance is routine instead of righteous, chronological instead of christological. It can appear that we are giving lip service to the Christian calendar so we can move on to the Hallmark calendar of Mother's Day, Graduation Sunday, and Memorial Day. Laurence Hull Stookey wrote, "The explosive force of the resurrection of the Lord is too vast to be contained within a celebration of one day." Revisiting the mystery over an extended period of time could encourage a deeper understanding of redemption, sanctification, salvation, renewal, and victory.[1]

For his congregation, Metropolitan Community United Methodist Church in New York City, William Marceus James (1913–2013) wrote, "Every day to us is Easter with its resurrection song. Even when life overwhelms us, Easter people sing this song."[2] If we are indeed Easter people, then protracting our celebration could help us remember that the transforming resurrection of the past also transforms our present and future.[3] How could we possibly fully grasp that truth in a single day?

TEAM DISCUSSION QUESTIONS

- If we are truly Easter people, then what is keeping us from expanding its celebration beyond a single day?

- How do we draw people in for special services without compromising our message or mission?

- How far is too far when promoting special Sundays or events?

- If our church doesn't celebrate Easter beyond a single Sunday, then how can we expand that celebration?

- If our church already celebrates Easter beyond a single Sunday, then how can we make those celebrations more impactful?

Chapter Seventeen
Songs That Preach

Preaching is the act of publicly proclaiming, teaching, or making something known. It exhorts, exposits, affirms, corrects, advocates, instructs, responds, and applies. The act of preaching communicates to us, for us, and through us. A sermon is preached to address and expound on the biblical, theological, doctrinal, and moral issues that impact every generation of every congregation each and every day. This connectional discourse is intended to challenge congregants to embrace these truths not only individually but also corporately.

So if the worship songs we select aren't complementing, resonating, and emulating these same characteristics, we probably need to select different songs. In other words, our songs must also preach.

- Our songs must reflect and respond to biblical text. Scripture must organically yield our songs instead of just fertilizing our own contrived language. We must constantly ask whether our song text is theologically sound and whether it affirms Scripture as central. Songs that do not provoke a response to the Word don't preach.

- Our songs must connect the word of God to the people of God. The dialogue of worship through our songs is formed when God's word is revealed. This revelation causes the people of God to respond through the prompting of the Holy Spirit. The result is a vertical conversation with God and horizontal communion with others. Our songs are the communally uttered words of God.

- Our songs must speak the gospel. Every song we sing must invite the congregation and guests to be a part of God's story through Jesus Christ. Our songs should help us understand what God is doing in and through our lives in the name of Jesus. Those songs must sing of the ongoing and enduring work of God through God's son, Jesus Christ.

- Our songs must be easy to follow and understand. If congregants can't follow our songs, then they have difficulty finding value in those songs and consequently can't be influenced and moved to respond to them and through them. Archaic or colloquial text should be filtered and melodies should be evaluated for singability.

- Our songs must be sung with integrity. Songs that preach communicate biblical, theological, and doctrinal truths. Our songs must be sung with the integrity of adequate external preparation that springs forth from internal conviction. It must be evident that our songs reflect what we believe and practice. Lives must replicate the texts we sing even when we aren't singing them. Songs sung with integrity engage and express biblical text with inspiration and conviction.

- Our songs must engage more than emotions. Scripture encourages us to love God with all our heart, soul, mind, and strength. Songs that just stir the emotions are incomplete; songs that do not begin from the depth of our soul are often trite; songs that don't require us to think are shallow; and songs that don't ask us to use our bodies as a living sacrifice in acts of service are selfish. Our songs must be sung from our entire being.

- Our songs must encourage action. Songs must not only inspire us through our hearing but also challenge us in our doing. They must not only inform but also engage the congregation. Singing our songs should cause us to ask what is going to change as a result of singing them. Singing in here is not enough until our songs also impact who we are out there. So the psalms, hymns, and spiritual songs we sing with gratitude in our hearts during our worship services must lead us to acts of service as worship. Then the word of Christ will live in us richly (Col 3:16).

TEAM DISCUSSION QUESTIONS

- What is our process for selecting worship songs, and what theological filters are used in that selection process?

- In what ways is it evident that Scripture is foundational to our song selections?

- How is our worship sending our congregation out to be worship doers and not just hearers?

- What standards do we have in place to ensure our songs are easy to understand and are singable?

- How can our songs encourage both a vertical relationship with God and a horizontal relationship with one another?

Chapter Eighteen
Modern Parable (Matthew 25:14-30)

The Master Worship Leader called three novices with various gifts, passions, and capabilities to lead worship in three churches with distinct characteristics and needs.

To the first novice worship leader the Master gave a worship band that included five stellar players on rhythm guitar, lead guitar, bass, drums, and keyboard.

To the second novice worship leader the Master gave an aging rockabilly guitarist and a high school cajon player.

And to the third novice worship leader the Master gave a piano-playing, long-retired kindergarten teacher to accompany hymns as long as they weren't in sharps.

So the Master entrusted the three novices to fulfill their unique worship callings in equally unique and sometimes-challenging church settings. The first novice realized his church wouldn't be able to begin more services or plant additional churches until new players were trained. So he encouraged his original band members to give lessons to younger players so they'd be available for new church plants and as substitute players throughout the year. He also began a school of the arts to cultivate younger players so his church could share some of those players with several smaller churches in their community.

The second novice quickly realized rockabilly didn't fit the worship culture of his congregation, so he used some of his worship budget to invest in more nuanced worship guitar lessons for his rockabilly guitarist and one of his rockabilly band associates. And since the high school cajon player would graduate in a year, he was asked to train a younger middle schooler to serve as his replacement upon graduation.

The third novice coasted, surfed ministry placement sites, went to conferences with his resume in hand, and waited for the Master to call him to a more favorable position.

The Master checked in with the three novices to see how they were responding to his unique call in their unique settings.

The novice with five players showed the Master how he had doubled the number of players originally entrusted to him. The Master commended him: "Good work! It's obvious you are not just a musician but also a leader of worship and worshippers. You are a worthy ministry servant who can be trusted with more."

The novice with two players showed the Master how he had invested in the skills of existing players and trained younger players for the future. The Master celebrated with him: "Great job! It's obvious you aren't doing this alone and value the calling and gifts of others. You are a model of servant leadership ready for additional responsibilities."

The novice with one player said, "Master, I know you have high worship standards and are not pleased with poor musicianship. Since no other players here at my church can live up to those expectations, I have been doing it all myself. I've been waiting for you to call me to another church with more skilled players who appreciate my musical prowess."

The Master was angry and disappointed at this response so he asked the third novice two final questions: "If you knew I was after high worship standards, then why haven't you been trying to achieve them where I called you with what I gave you? And if you haven't been giving your best to this place where I called you now and have been saving it for where you hope I will call you next, then why would I want to?"

TEAM DISCUSSION QUESTIONS

- How are we doing at stewarding those worship gifts with which we have been entrusted?

- If we want great worship leaders in the future, then what are some ways we should be investing in not-yet-great worship leaders in the present?

- What process would we need to go through to secure additional budget money to help some of our players with additional lessons?

- What standards do we need to put in place to make sure our worship never coasts?

Chapter Nineteen
Gotta Serve Somebody

Sunday worship is both the culmination and commencement of the worship week. *Commencement* means a beginning or a start and *culmination* means an end or an arrival at a final stage. When considering these definitions with regard to Sunday worship, what seems mutually exclusive is actually collectively exhaustive. Is the Sunday worship service the commencement of the worship week? Yes! Is the Sunday worship service the culmination of the worship week? Yes!

As a commencement, the Sunday service sings our congregations out. The worship when we gather may be great, but until it impacts those we come into contact with when we disperse, it's incomplete. As a culmination, the Sunday service sings our congregations in. Gathered worship is then a continuation and celebration of the worship that has already been occurring during the week through sacrificial acts of service. So Sunday is the day we both gather them for worship and disperse them to worship.

A couple of decades ago I was conducting the last Saturday morning rehearsal before our choir and orchestra presented their Christmas music the next day in our services. We needed six hours of rehearsal but only had three, so the stress was high and levity low. Right in the middle of rehearsing one of the songs, a man entered the worship center behind me, distracting the players and singers. I stopped the song to address the interruption and regain control of rehearsal.

It was obvious from his appearance that this man's needs were benevolent ones. He was there to request help with food for his family, fuel for their car, and firewood to heat their home. Since he had recently lost his job, he was also hoping our church could help with Christmas gifts for his children. I responded to his request by saying, "We're in the middle of preparing for a special Christmas worship service tomorrow at church, so we won't have time to help you right now. But if you'll come by our offices on Monday, we'll see if we can get you some assistance." He never returned.

Mark Labberton wrote, "Worship can name a Sunday gathering of God's people, but it also includes how we treat those around us, how we spend our money, and how we care for the lost and the oppressed. Worship can encompass every dimension of our lives."[1] I often wonder how much more impactful our Christmas worship services on that Sunday evening might have been if I had taken a few moments to serve as an act of worship on that Saturday morning.

We sing psalms and hymns and spiritual songs as an expression of our desire to know Jesus, but the Jesus we want to know is the sanitized Jesus who looks a lot like us. Despite God's word to the contrary, we think that we can say we love God yet hate our neighbor, neglect the widow, forget the orphan, fail to visit the prisoner, ignore the oppressed. When we do this, our worship becomes a lie to God.[2]

Serving others reminds us that the sermons we have prepared and songs we have selected may not be the most important act of worship this week. Serving others is one of those actions we take to ensure that worship continues when we leave our services. We spend so much time leading church services as an act of worship that we often neglect to lead the church in service as an act of worship too. Worship as service will never be completely realized until we can say every Sunday, "Worship has left the building." God is looking for a worship lifestyle that rights wrongs, cares for the poor, rejects injustice, and embraces generosity. Worship that comes from a community that doesn't model those characteristics turns the beautiful melodies we've just sung into something discordant.[3]

TEAM DISCUSSION QUESTIONS

- What could occur as we lead gathered worship on Sunday if we have served together as a team during the week?

- How can we better balance our time between our worship services and worship as service?

- In what ways can we ensure the songs we sing on Sunday are also evident in the lives we lead the rest of the week?

- What service ministry might we adopt together as a team?

Chapter Twenty

Chapter Twenty
First Corinthians 13 for Worship Leaders

If I sing like my favorite worship artist, but do not have love,

    I am just a loud kick drum or cheap crash cymbal.

If I have the gift of creative verbal transitions

    and understand the mystery and knowledge of chord charts and choir scores,

    and if I have the faith that can move the emotions of an entire congregation,

    but do not have love, I am nothing.

If I give the old sound system to a poor congregation,

    install the new one all by myself,

    and then post it on social media so all my friends will know,

    but do not have love, I won't get any likes.

Love is patient with a congregation that is slow to change,

    love is kind to the tech team.

Love doesn't envy the size of another church,

    it doesn't brag during the worship pastor's lunch meeting,

    or incessantly promote itself on YouTube.

Love doesn't publicly complain about its players or pastor,

    or use its present ministry to climb the ladder toward a future ministry.

It doesn't lose its temper when the lead guitarist misses the bridge,

or keep track of how many times it has happened before.

Love is not happy with worship team spiritual apathy

so it encourages a culture of mutual accountability.

It always protects confidentialities, always trusts the team members,

always hopes biblical worship is central, and always rehearses just one more time.

Love never coasts.

But where there are creative verbal transitions, they will cease;

where there are beautiful voices to sing amazing songs, they will be silent;

where there is musical knowledge, it will pass away.

For we kind-of know and can kind-of talk about worship,

but when perfect worship occurs, the kind-of will disappear.

When I was a child, I sang childish songs.

When I became a man, I traded childish songs for adult songs . . .
but still just songs.

For now we see hazily, as through the mist of a fog machine.

But soon the haze will evaporate and the room will be completely clear.

Now I kind-of know;

then I will fully know, even as I am fully known.

Until that time, until we fully know, we must do three things:

Have faith that God will help us.

Hope that we are getting it right.

And love God and one another.

As worship leaders, love often seems to be the hardest. But it is also the greatest.

TEAM DISCUSSION QUESTIONS

- How do we foster a culture of excellence and accountability but still with an attitude of benevolence?

- In what ways is it evident to the congregation that those who lead them love not only God but also one another?

- How do we respond to one another when mistakes occur?

- How can we convey to the congregation that our tech team members are also worship leaders?

Chapter Twenty-One
Hooked on a Feeling

If we are waiting on a feeling for worship to occur, then it may never occur. Worship contingent on a musical experience that just stirs the emotions may not be worship, but instead nostalgia or novelty. Nostalgia is sentimental remembrance of previous times that stir happy or meaningful personal recollections. It can cause a congregation to romanticize, idealize, and even embellish past experiences. The result is an attempt to re-create divine moments, events, or even seasons based almost completely on the feelings originally stirred.

Novelty is the quality of being new, original, or unusual just to be new, original, or unusual. A novelty entertains for a short period of time until another novelty surfaces. College freshmen enjoy the novelty of independence until they have to do their own laundry. A child's birthday present is novel until he opens the next one. Novelty as it relates to worship can cause a congregation to over-innovate, over-stimulate, and over-imitate. Each Sunday then becomes an exercise in surpassing the creativity of the previous one.

When congregations gather for worship they may be hooked on a feeling stirred by nostalgia or novelty instead of spirit and truth worship. If those feelings are not elicited because they don't know or don't particularly like the songs, they can even leave the worship service believing that worship couldn't and didn't occur.

We learn from Scripture that we were created and sustained so that we can offer our worship to God alone. When the scribes asked Jesus which commandments were the greatest, he replied, "And you must love the Lord your God with all your heart, with all your being, with all your mind, and with all your strength" (Mark 12:30).

- *In worship we love God with all our HEART.*

The heart is often the symbol of our emotions. Worship is indeed emotional, but emotions alone can be shallow, especially when limited to the single emotion of happiness. Our heart reminds us that sorrow, pain, grief, fear, loneliness, lament, and even despair are also authentic worship emotions.

- *In worship we love God with all our BEING.*

True worship doesn't begin with what we do; it begins with who we are in response to who God is and what God has done. Spirit and truth worship begins in the depth of our soul. What occurs in our soul is then manifested in our worship actions. When we invert this, our worship becomes religion instead of response.

- *In worship we love God with all our MIND.*

The mind allows us to approach worship with knowledge, insight, reason, memory, creativity, inquiry, imagination, and even doubt. The Apostle Paul stated that spiritual transformation occurs through the renewing of our minds. Offering our prayers, reading and hearing Scripture, remembering at the Lord's Supper Table, and singing our songs without engaging our minds lead to thoughtless worship.

- *In worship we love God with all our STRENGTH.*

Worship without strength is often passive. Since liturgy means the work of the people, it is something we actually do, not something that is done for us. When we offer our bodies as a living sacrifice, we are responding to God's workmanship by doing good works. Loving God with all our strength is the external expression of the internal impression of loving God with all our heart, soul, and mind.

- *In worship we love God by loving our NEIGHBOR.*

It doesn't matter how good our worship is in here; it is still incomplete until it also includes how we treat our neighbors out there. We must lead, model, and teach the church to worship not only when we gather with our church family but also when we scatter back to our neighborhoods.

TEAM DISCUSSION QUESTIONS

- Can we recall any recent instances during which nostalgia or novelty seemed to surface in our worship-planning and worship-leading?

- How can we help our congregation move from focusing on worship likes and dislikes to focusing on worship that begins from the depth of their being?

- How can we help the congregation focus less on us and more on God?

- How would we actually know if we are selecting songs just because of how they make us feel?

Chapter Twenty-Two
Buyer's Remorse

In an effort to initiate worship change, leaders often rush into doing anything different than what they think is not working now. Failing to initiate worship change when change is necessary can cause a congregation to get stuck. But initiating those changes without appropriate preparation could cause congregational buyer's remorse.

FIVE KEYS TO AVOID BUYER'S REMORSE

- *Select the appropriate score.*

A score is the tool used by a composer, conductor, or analyst that shows all the parts of an ensemble, enabling the experienced reader to "hear" what the composition will sound like. The score is the focus, outline, containment, and limitations of the considered change. Even though a score has framework limitations, it is still open to the interpretation of the conductor and players.[1]

Selecting the appropriate score for change requires preparation, prayer, discernment, study, observation, and buy-in before actually initiating a change. Andy Stanley wrote, "Designing and implementing a strategy for change is a waste of time until you have discovered and embraced the current reality. If you don't know where you really are, it is impossible to get to where you need to be. What you don't know can kill you."[2]

- *Rehearse before you perform.*

Rehearsing a change is actively soliciting buy-in from congregants with unique gifts, perspectives, and abilities. The pain of transition is amplified when leaders discount congregational members as uninformed, incapable of grasping the theological implications of change, or so rooted in their old identity and behavior that they are unwilling to think in new ways.

Rehearsing change creates an environment in which individuals realize their wisdom is an essential part of what is being created. Shared vision allows a congregation to consider the various perspectives and molds them within the framework of the score. It then creates a unified ensemble ready for the final presentation. Peter Senge describes shared vision as "creating a *relational child*, a unique future that will only emerge with shared dialogue and cooperative implementation."[3]

• *Set a healthy tempo.*

Tempo is the relative speed at which a composition is to be played. Rehearsal gives a congregation time to set the proper *tempo* for change. What might appear to a leader to be the quickest and most direct route for worship change may seem reckless to members of the congregation who have the same goals but are more comfortable taking safer or slower routes.

Ignoring signals of caution can create conflict, sabotage trust, leave those we lead in our wake, and cause us to retrace our steps. What was intended to accelerate the pace may in fact slow it. The tempo established during rehearsal can kill a composition, or it can promote its success.

• *Use modulation in key changes.*

Modulation is the process of moving from one key to another. The essential word is *process*. Change is a process, not a one-time event.[4]

Modulation offers a congregation a less painful transition by allowing time for them to come to terms with their new worship changes. Jumping from one key to another without the process of modulation is abrupt and jarring, leaving the congregation stunned and frustrated. Ironically, one of the key components of a successful modulation is dissonance.

Dissonance will occur in the change process and cannot be ignored or it will surface again. Resolving dissonance in the modulation process releases the tension of moving from the previous to the new. Transformation takes time, and the process is just as important as the end result.

• *Perform—initiate the change.*

Performance is the act of presenting, of doing something successfully and using knowledge as distinguished from merely possessing it. Andy Stanley tells the story of the early days of the Civil War, when northern generals were so focused on avoiding casualties and embarrassing losses that they would miss strategic opportunities. They spent more time exercising the troops than they did engaging the enemy. Stanley wrote, "Simply recognizing the need for change does not define leadership. The leader is the one who has the courage to act on what he sees."[5]

Leadership is not about making change decisions on your own, but it is about owning those decisions once they are made. Stanley also said, "While the average man or woman fears stepping out into a new opportunity, the leader fears missing out on a new opportunity."[6]

Initiating worship change without planning and serious reflection often causes unnecessary buyer's remorse. Faithful leaders successfully open their congregations to new concepts by accenting what they are now doing well, by giving those congregants time to consider what they might do better, and by involving them all throughout the process.

TEAM DISCUSSION QUESTIONS

- Can we recall any instances in which worship changes were indeed necessary but were implemented too quickly? How about too slowly?

- How do we determine if worship change is necessary, and who should be involved in that discernment process?

- What should occur before we can be certain it is an appropriate time to initiate changes?

- How might we rehearse those changes with our congregation without causing unnecessary anxiety?

Chapter Twenty-Three

Conversational Narcissists

We are created in God's image, not God in ours. When we worship we must acknowledge that we aren't starting the conversation. Instead, God began the dialogue and is inviting us to join it. If we create worship just to accommodate our needs, then the god we worship looks a lot like us.

Our worship proclaims, enacts, and sings God's story.[1] If our worship is truly in spirit and truth, then it must reflect who God is, not necessarily just what we want. When we focus on what we need, deserve, and prefer, the attention is always on us. But when we focus on what God desires, the attention is always on God.

Conversational narcissism is what sociologist Charles Derber calls the constant shifting of the conversation away from others and back to us. Derber wrote, "One conversationalist transforms another's topic into one pertaining to himself through the persistent use of the shift-response."[2] Shift-response is taking the topic of conversation initiated by another and shifting its focus to our own selfish interests. We've all been involved in those conversations that have been hijacked by someone who makes their own story seem more dramatic, humorous, or emotional than all others. A conversation that began with others ends up focused on them.

Conversational narcissism is manifested in worship when we take the topic and shift its focus to a topic of our own choosing. Instead of worship focused on God and God's story, it is focused on me and my story.[3] Shifting the topic of our worship can also shift the object of our worship. When those shifts occur, the conversation is no longer initiated by or focused on the worshipped but instead on the worshipper. In his essay "Meditation in a Toolshed," C. S. Lewis illustrated the difference between just seeing something as an outsider and actually seeing or looking along something as an insider:

I was standing today in the dark toolshed. The sun was shining outside and through the crack at the top of the door there came a sunbeam. From where I stood that beam of light, with the specks of dust floating in it, was the most striking thing in the place. Everything else was almost pitch-black. I was seeing the beam, not seeing things by it. Then I moved, so that the beam fell on my eyes. Instantly the whole previous picture vanished. I saw no toolshed, and (above all) no beam. Instead I saw, framed in the irregular cranny at the top of the door, green leaves moving on the branches of a tree outside and beyond that, 90 odd million miles away, the sun. Looking along the beam, and looking at the beam are very different experiences.[4]

When we stand outside of the beam and expect it to move where we are, the god we worship looks like us. We believe that the beam is there for our sake instead of our being there for its sake. Then the object of our worship (God and God's story) is transferred to an object of our own choosing (us and our story). Harold Best wrote, "Idolatry is the difference between walking in the light and creating our own light to walk in."[5] But when we step into the beam and look along that beam, we don't just see God, we also see what God wants us to see. Then our worship is no longer shaped by what we want or feel like we've earned, but instead is shaped by who God is and what God has done.

TEAM DISCUSSION QUESTIONS

- How can we help our congregation step into God's story instead of expecting God to step into ours?

- Since we get to select what occurs in worship each week, how can we make sure we aren't selecting worship elements just to accommodate our own needs?

- Are there any recent examples where it seems like we asked God to move the beam where we are?

- What worship elements could we introduce to help our congregants transform from selfish to selfless worshippers?

Chapter Twenty-Four

Starting a Fire from Scratch

In the 2000 movie *Cast Away*, Tom Hanks played a man named Chuck Noland, who was the lone survivor of a plane crash on an uninhabited island. Early in the movie, Noland realized he couldn't survive without fire and offered us a glimpse of his resolve, despair, anger, and even humor as he labored over trying to start a fire from scratch.

Worship leaders can experience similar emotions when they are expected to light a fire each Sunday with the opening song. And even though congregants might not have done anything to help stir those embers during the week themselves, how easily they can blame the music or musicians when the spark is not there.

Worship leaders and the songs they sing can't light a fire in us or usher us into the presence of God; the death and resurrection of Jesus already has. When we ascribe that power to earthly leaders, we begin to see their leadership as something that is meritorious or efficacious, meaning their actions are praised for what they can produce.[1] Those worship actions can indeed prompt, exhort, encourage, and remind us of God's presence, but they can't create or lead us into it.

God's presence isn't a physical place we attend or an emotional plane we achieve; we don't go to it, sing it into existence, light it, or usher people into it. Instead, we have confidence to enter that holy place only by the blood of Jesus. And as our mediator, Jesus is not only the object of our worship but also the facilitator of it.

If we are not careful, our actions can imply that time-and-place worship is the primary—if not only—venue for worship, while the remainder of our life falls into another category.[2] Every Sunday can end up being a frustrating exercise in trying to start a fire from scratch or usher congregants into the presence of God.

Because of the laborious task of fire-starting, ancient nomadic people began to use earthenware vessels called fire pots. They would carry embers or slow-burning fires in these pots with them as they traveled from one location to another. Just by adding small amounts of kindling for fuel, they could keep those mini fires alive, enabling them to quickly ignite larger fires when they united as a group for their evening camps.

John the Evangelist wrote, "This is the message that we have heard from him and announce to you: 'God is light and there is no darkness in him at all.' If we claim, 'We have fellowship with him,' and live in the darkness, we are lying and do not act truthfully. But if we live in the light in the same way as he is in the light, we have fellowship with each other, and the blood of Jesus, his Son, cleanses us from every sin" (1 John 1:5-7).

Instead of seeing worship as a new fire to start each week, what if we saw it as a flame or light that can be taken with us? Then it could continue as we leave the service. It could happen in our homes, at our schools, through our work, and in our culture. It couldn't be contained in a single location, context, culture, style, artistic expression, or vehicle of communication. Consequently, instead of depending on our worship leaders to start the fire from scratch when we gather each week, they could just help us fan those flames that already exist.

TEAM DISCUSSION QUESTIONS

- What changes must we make in how we lead if our congregation expects us to light a worship fire from scratch each week?

- If continuous worship is our goal, then how do we train our congregation to take that worship spark with them when they leave?

- What might our worship look like when we gather on Sunday if our congregants have been continuous worshippers during the week?

- What language could we use to send worshippers out for continuous worship?

Chapter Twenty-Five
Is Hallmark Planning Your Services?

Some congregations and even entire denominations have not embraced the Christian calendar as foundational to their worship-planning and implementation out of concern that it is too rigid, routine, or orthodox. In their desire to be nonliturgical, they have in fact created their own liturgy framed by Hallmark or denominational and civic calendars.

The desire for worship creativity has caused some congregations to look elsewhere, believing annual celebrations promote monotony and conformity. But Timothy Carson wrote, "Exactly the opposite may be true. Because it has stood the test of time, it may be sufficiently deep to allow me to swim more deeply in it. Because it is repeated, I have another chance, today, to go where I could not go yesterday."[1]

In the Middle Ages the church calendar was filled with such a multitude of saints' days that the value of festivals such as Christmas, Easter, and Pentecost was lost. In response, some of the Reformers eliminated the entire church year. Other Protestants responded similarly, and in the sixteenth century the Puritans rejected even Christmas as a festival day.[2]

As Protestant congregations started again to commemorate special days, they focused on cultural and denominational calendars instead of on the Christian calendar. As the antitheses to what was considered Catholic, these civic days were given as much or more credibility as the days of the Christian calendar. But some congregations who avoided the Christian calendar were affirming annual observances whose foundations were not biblically grounded.[3]

I love, appreciate, and revere my family. I am grateful I get to be their husband and dad. I think about them often and can't imagine life without them. Our story is something I enjoy celebrating and telling others about every chance I get. As a result of that gratitude, what if I used the worship service this Sunday just to exalt my family? Instead of worshipping God that day, what if I planned the entire service to celebrate and sing the praises of my family?

If idolatry is extreme devotion to anyone or anything that isn't God, then replacing the cross with our mothers, fathers, graduates, or the flag as the primary symbol of our worship on any given Sunday could cause us to stray into idol territory. God's story and our response to that story transcend cultural and denominational calendars.

Harold Best wrote, "There is one fundamental fact about worship: at this very moment, and for as long as this world endures, everybody inhabiting it is bowing down and serving something or someone—an artifact, a person, an institution, an idea, a spirit, or God through Christ."[4] Best continued with, "All worship outside the worship of God through Christ Jesus is idolatrous."[5]

God has placed each one of our congregations in a unique cultural and national context. Worshipping while giving consideration to those contexts is one of the exciting challenges for a modern church. As long as Christian worship is our starting point it will provide us with the opportunity to take up that challenge without compromising our biblical and theological foundations.[6] Why couldn't we celebrate Mother's Day, Graduation Sunday, and Memorial Day in the same seasons as Ascension Day and Pentecost? Without ignoring one or the other, it is possible to converge holidays significant to our civic and denominational calendars with those Christian holidays significant to the kingdom.

TEAM DISCUSSION QUESTIONS

- What days or seasons in the Christian calendar haven't we been observing that we could add to our worship calendar?

- How can we incorporate cultural, denominational, and Christian calendar observances within our worship service?

- How can we move away from observing holidays that are causing us to take our focus from the worship of God, while still being sensitive to the emotional connection those days have for our congregation?

Chapter Twenty-Six
Measure Twice, Cut Once

Baseball utility players are prized for their versatility even though they don't have enough talent to crack the starting lineup. They are usually excellent players but not quite good enough to help carry the team from a starting position. A utility player is more supplemental than foundational to the success of each game. He waits on the bench until the manager needs him to fill any of a variety of positions in the lineup.

Prayer has been relegated to the role of a worship service utility player. It is often plugged into worship service holes when the starters (songs and sermons) need a break. Instead of a foundational conversation with God as an act of worship, prayer is often a supplemental extra used to fill in, transition, or connect. Prayer has been demoted to the role of a worship service starter, stuffer, and stopper, or jack-of-all-trades service element. It serves as the seventh-inning stretch before the sermon; it breaks up the song sets when keys aren't relative; it moves the worship band on the platform; and it allows the pastor to discreetly make her way up the aisle to shake hands after the service.

Maybe we are singing more and praying less because our prayers during the worship service are not that deep. Song texts have been parsed, prayed over, and practiced, while our prayers are often played by ear. Our spontaneous prayers may be sincere, but they're often not very profound. Spontaneity needs to be balanced by careful preparation and forethought. Public praying needs to be supported by private praying. Those who publicly lead in prayer must be well experienced in prayer. It is difficult to lead others where you haven't been yourself. Spontaneity has to arise from a profound experience of prayer.[1]

Maybe we are singing more and praying less because prayer is such an easy language to fake. We can, in fact, pretend to pray, use the words of prayer, practice forms of prayer, assume postures of prayer, acquire a reputation for prayer, and never pray.[2]

"Measure twice, cut once" is a woodworking idiom that encourages us to plan and prepare for something of value in a careful and thorough manner before acting. In other words, think before you speak; don't shoot from the hip; set a guard over my mouth; keep watch over the door that is our lips (Ps 141:3).

The result of ill-prepared praying is often a long-winded circular discourse. Those with prayer responsibilities could learn a valuable lesson from microblogging sites such as Twitter whose success is based on succinct but also persuasive information. Character limitations force users to formulate a mental outline of what is essential to say and how it needs to be said. They measure twice before cutting once.

Maybe we are singing more and praying less because we actually require our soloists, choirs, orchestras, worship teams, and bands to rehearse ahead of time, but most of the offerings from our pray-ers are casual, impromptu, spontaneous, and sometimes even shallow. Hughes Oliphant Old wrote, "For many generations American Protestants have prized spontaneity in public prayer. One has to admit, however, that the spontaneous prayer one often hears in public worship is an embarrassment to the tradition. It all too often lacks content. It may be sincere, but sometimes it is not very profound."[3] If worship service prayer preparations were as stringent as those for our musical offerings, then maybe we would consider singing less in order to pray more. Then maybe our worship service prayers would again be considered foundational instead of supplemental.

TEAM DISCUSSION QUESTIONS

- How can we transform our worship service prayers from starters, stuffers, and stoppers to a divine conversation with God?

- What training could we initiate to better prepare those who lead our worship service prayers?

- If we are asking the same few people to lead our prayers, then how can we expand that list to include multiple generations, genders, and cultures?

- How do we ensure prayer is foundational instead of supplemental to our worship services?

- What can we do to expand a healthier culture of prayer outside our services so it might impact the worship inside our services?

Chapter Twenty-Seven
Sing Me into Heaven

The purpose of our worship service music isn't to prepare our hearts for something else. It doesn't just set the table for the sermon. Paul exhorted the saints at Ephesus to be filled with the Spirit by speaking to each other with psalms, hymns, and spiritual songs (Eph 5:19). It doesn't sound like Paul thought worship music was only a supporting role.

Teaching proclaims or makes something known by precept, example, and experience. It exhorts, instructs, exposits, and applies. And it communicates to us and through us.

Admonition urges us not just to hear but to do. It reproves, advises, and counsels in order to correct our thinking. It encourages us to right what is wrong in order to redirect our attitudes and motives.

Our worship songs won't be seen as just service starters if they quicken the conscience through the holiness of God, feed the mind with the truth of God, purge the imagination by the beauty of God, open the heart to the love of God, and devote the will to the purpose of God.[1] The theology we sing is not just an appetizer before the main course when it teaches and admonishes us to be doers and not just hearers.

I recently attended a memorial service for a friend and former volunteer music minister. "Sing me into heaven" was his final request as his musical family gathered around his hospital bed in his last hours of life. That grieving family honored his wishes by recalling and singing every sacred song they could remember. What a comforting way to enter into eternity.

Hope can be found when we realize we are never singing those sacred songs alone. The prophet Zephaniah wrote, "The LORD your God is in your midst—a warrior bringing victory. He will create calm with his love; he will rejoice over you with singing" (Zeph 3:17). And Scripture tells us that Jesus as our high priest is seated at the right side of the throne of majesty and is interceding for us (Heb 8:1-2; 2:12). Even when our songs are choked with emotion, God is singing over us and Jesus is interceding for us.

Darryl Tippen wrote, "Without music we are left with talk. The trouble with talk is that it tends to position the speaker in a place of power. It puts one in charge, which can border on a dangerous conceit when it comes to reporting on the Almighty. A different, humbler posture of spirit emerges in worship and song. When we are singing, there is a sense that we are not in charge."[2]

Singing is a language that allows us to embody our love for our creator. It is a means God has given us to communicate our deepest affections, to have our thoughts exquisitely shaped, and to have our spirits braced for the boldest of obedience.[3]

Our bodies, emotions, and intellect are mysteriously connected when we sing. Christian songs are effective because they implant the truths of the faith in our hearts, not just in our heads. They rehearse the stories of Scripture. In word and sound we experience Gethsemane, the cross, and the Resurrection. We remember our sinfulness, our need for redemption, our duty to our neighbor, and the promise of eternal life.[4]

With that understanding, "sing me into heaven" becomes not only a final request but also an ongoing challenge for worship leaders and congregants each time they align their spirits and voices in congregational song.

TEAM DISCUSSION QUESTIONS

- What can we do differently in our worship services to help our congregation understand music as more than an appetizer before the sermon?

- According to Scripture, who is actually our worship leader?

- How do we evaluate our songs to ensure they are faithfully rehearsing the stories of Scripture?

- How can we move our song sets from just communicating *to* us to also communicating *through* us?

Chapter Twenty-Eight
Scriptureless

By limiting Scripture to a single reading prior to the pastoral exhortation, we may be unwittingly implying that we are placing a higher level of credibility in the exhortation than in the Word itself. It may then convey a lack of trust in the very Word professed to be foundational to our faith, doctrines, and practices. If Scripture can't stand on its own, then we can't possibly prop it up with our own words.

Robert Webber in *Ancient-Future Worship* wrote, "We are nourished in worship by Jesus Christ, who is the living Word disclosed to us in the Scriptures, the written Word of God. In spite of all the emphasis we evangelicals have placed on the importance of the Bible, there seems to be a crisis of the Word among us."[1]

Congregations continue to struggle in their understanding of spirit and truth worship by maximizing music and depending on it alone to encourage worship renewal. At the same time those congregations often minimize the very root from which our songs must spring. John Frame offers two truths that highlight the value of God's word in our worship: "First, where God's Word is, God is. We should never take God's Word for granted. To hear the Word of God is to meet with God himself. Second, where God is, the Word is. We should not seek to have an experience with God which bypasses or transcends his Word."[2]

The dialogue of worship is formed when God's word is revealed. This revelation causes worshippers to respond through the prompting of the Holy Spirit (1 Cor 2:12-15; 1 Thess 1:5). The result is a vertical conversation with God and horizontal communion with others. This dialogue develops a community that congregations have been desperately trying to create and re-create through their songs alone.

Some of the crisis of the Word is a result of our standing over the Bible and reading God's narrative from outside instead of standing within the narrative and reading Scripture from the inside.[3] Reading Scripture as insiders helps us realize the text is not just describing someone else's story in history but also describing the story of my life, my hope, my joy, my sin, and my journey away from and to God.[4]

As an elementary school teacher, my wife often reads or tells stories to her students to enhance auditory learning, encourage creativity, promote informational development, and advance knowledge. With imagination beyond my comprehension she is able to create stories and insert the names of her classroom children into the narrative, considering the personality and nature of each child. This narrative approach to reading and telling moves the children beyond just *hearing* the words to actually *living inside* those words.

When Scripture is read, when it is illuminated in our preaching, when it is incorporated into our prayers of thanksgiving and lament, when it frames the celebration of the Lord's Supper, and when we sing its text in a unified voice, Scripture becomes a means by which we are gathered into the body of the living Lord.[5]

Scripture must be foundational to our songs, sermons, prayers, verbal transitions, and even ministry announcements. It must be frequently, variously, generationally, and culturally read and allowed to stand on its own. When that occurs, our congregations will leave *in-here* worship, with the text in their hearts and on their lips, for nonstop worship *out there*.

TEAM DISCUSSION QUESTIONS

- How often are we reading Scripture in our worship services beyond the text for pastoral exhortation?

- How might we encourage our congregation to not only hear the words of Scripture but also live inside those words?

- Who usually reads Scripture in our services? Are we enlisting multiple generations, genders, and cultures as readers?

- What filters should we put in place to help us determine if Scripture is primary instead of secondary in our worship services?

Chapter Twenty-Nine
Death Zone

The death zone is a mountaineering reference to the altitude above a certain point where the oxygen level is no longer high enough to sustain human life. It has been generally recognized as any altitude above eight thousand meters or twenty-six thousand feet. Spending time in an oxygen-deprived atmosphere can cause climbers to make irrational decisions due to the deterioration of their physical and mental capacities. An extended stay in the death zone without the proper safeguards will ultimately lead to a loss of consciousness and death.

Leading worship from the death zone is attempting to sustain an elevated level or pace that has the potential to jeopardize your family, your ministry, and your health. Recognizing and acknowledging the following warning signs helps establish safeguards before you no longer have the capacity to replenish your reserves.

- *You are trying to do it alone.*

  You probably have enough talent to succeed alone for a time. A time will come, however, when the inherent risks of trying to do it on your own will cause you to fail alone.

- *You aren't taking care of yourself.*

  To sustain effective worship leadership, you must learn to take care of yourself spiritually, emotionally, and physically. If you aren't doing it, no one else will.

- ### *You are ignoring your family.*

Loving your family means spending time with them. Don't ignore family in the name of ministry, since taking care of your family is ministry. You'll never recover missed opportunities with your spouse and children.

- ### *You aren't setting appropriate boundaries.*

Boundaries are spiritual, familial, professional, emotional, physical, mental, ethical, and relational countermeasures or limits. They are precautionary gauges put in place to ward off impending dangers. Boundaries give you permission to say no.

- ### *You aren't preparing for the future.*

Worship leaders who ignore the steps to recalibrate often find themselves only prepared to lead a church or ministry that no longer exists. What you once learned is not nearly enough to sustain you for your entire ministry. Doing ministry in this zone is usually a slow death, but it is still terminal.

God never promised those of us who lead worship that we would always be happy, revered, loved, encouraged, appreciated, followed, and successful. God did, however, promise that God would never leave us or abandon us. We can say with confidence, "Be strong! Be fearless! Don't be afraid and don't be scared by your enemies, because the LORD your God is the one who marches with you. He won't let you down, and he won't abandon you" (Deut 31:6; see also Heb 13:5-6).

Sailors in the eighteenth and nineteenth centuries superstitiously believed that certain tattoos brought good luck and helped them avert disaster at sea. So the letters H-O-L-D F-A-S-T were tattooed with one letter on each finger. The tattoo was believed to protect a sailor whose life depended on holding fast to a rope on the ship's deck or while working aloft in the ship's rigging. The writer of the book of Hebrews wrote the same words, not as superstitious chance but with a genuine heart, with the certainty that our faith gives us: "Let's hold on to the confession of our hope without wavering, because the one who made the promises is reliable" (Heb 10:23).

When it seems like all of the oxygen has been sucked out of the room and you can't seem to catch your breath, hold fast because the God who calls us will also sustain us. Hold fast because God remembers where we are and where God called us. Hold fast in full assurance that God knows what we are going through. Hold fast because our ministry life depends on it.

TEAM DISCUSSION QUESTIONS

- How can we help our worship leaders balance ministry and family when we don't have people to fill in for them when they need a break?

- What safeguards do we have in place to help protect our leaders spiritually, emotionally, and physically?

- Since Sunday is not a Sabbath for our worship leaders, when is?

- What policies could we put in place to help our leaders set and keep appropriate boundaries?

Chapter Thirty
Getting Rid of Volunteers

In the late 1990s, the Gallup organization performed a research study asking more than a million people from a variety of companies and organizations what the most talented employees need from their workplace. Their results indicated that even though talented employees might have initially joined a company because of a variety of incentives, they actually stayed and were more productive because of their relationship with their immediate leaders. The researchers then asked more than eighty thousand business leaders how they find, focus, and keep talented employees. They discovered that asking employees to respond to twelve simple questions developed through their research could help them measure the strength of a workplace.[1]

Are you even asking critical questions to determine why your worship volunteers are or aren't engaged? Part of our problem with retention is that we don't often ask any questions at all—that is, until it is too late. Maybe if we asked our volunteers similar questions their responses would help us adjust our culture so they will succeed and stay.[2]

I have adapted the language of those twelve Gallup questions to fit a worship-leading context for you and your worship volunteers to consider:

1. Do I know what is expected of me in our worship ministry?

2. Do I have the materials and equipment I need to do this ministry well?

3. Do I have the opportunity to do what I do best every time I serve?

4. Have I received recognition or praise for doing good work in the last seven days?

5. Does my leader or someone else in our worship ministry seem to care about me as a person?

6. Is there someone in this ministry who encourages my development?

7. Do my opinions seem to count?

8. Does the mission of our worship ministry make me feel like my contribution is important?

9. Are my co-volunteers and leaders committed to quality?

10. Do I have a close friend in our worship ministry?

11. In the last six months has someone in this ministry talked to me about my progress?

12. During this last year have I had opportunities in our worship ministry to learn and grow?[3]

Is it possible the reason you're having a hard time retaining worship volunteers isn't their lack of commitment or conviction but instead something you as their leaders are or aren't doing? If you want to constantly replace volunteers in your band, worship team, choir, or tech team, then try some of the following:

• *Compare them with others.*

Are you critical when volunteers can't imitate a worship model you consider successful? Is it evident you are disappointed when they don't measure up to your expectations? How well would comparisons like that work in your marriage?

• *Come to rehearsals unprepared.*

Your lack of preparation indicates either laziness or arrogance. Both reasons convey that your time is more valuable than theirs. And being an artist and a leader doesn't give you permission for either one.

- ## *Treat them like backup musicians.*

Why wouldn't they assume expendability if you treat them like they are just the backup band? You might have enough talent to succeed on your own, but that is not what you have been called to do.

- ## *Consider them as just volunteers.*

Serving as a worship volunteer is their response to a divine invitation. Since volunteers serve because of calling, they should never be treated as just volunteers filling a vacancy. Your worship volunteers are instead ministers fulfilling their mission.

- ## *Never affirm them publicly or privately.*

Yes, it's true their service is for God, not you. But they still need you to affirm them regularly, intentionally, and meaningfully. They need to know their contributions are fulfilling expectations, are valued multilaterally, and are making an eternal difference.

- ## *Never give them a break.*

Don't forget volunteers also have jobs and families when you are scheduling them for multiple services every week and rehearsals that run long. Enlist a large enough pool of volunteers for a rotation to give them a break.

- ## *Make all worship decisions for them.*

Leading like you alone have the ability, creativity, and even the right to make all worship decisions means you are guarding your status and not leading others. Entitlement and control may achieve compliance for a short time but rarely the buy-in of a long-term commitment.

Legend is told that when Achilles was an infant, his mother dipped him into the river Styx to make him immortal. But since she held him by one heel, that spot didn't touch the water so it remained mortal or vulnerable. An Achilles' heel is now idiomatic for a point of weakness or deficiency in spite of an overall strength. If ignored or disregarded, that weak spot could lead to failure.

As worship leaders, we're not immune to our own Achilles' heels when relating to our worship teams. Relational instead of musical deficiencies seem to be at the root of most of those vulnerable places. And yet, we often invest the majority of our time and attention trying to improve musically. Arrogance and aloofness are two of those Achilles' heels that could lead to conflict or even failure.

Instead of a desire to be revered, maybe our worship-leading prayer should be, "Lord, deliver us from the need to always have the last word." Arrogance can even suggest that what we lead and how well we lead it are more important than those whom we lead. Aloofness is that state of being distant, remote, withdrawn, and unapproachable. It's difficult to foster deep worship-leading relationships with our teams if we are trying to lead from that set-apart artistic zone. If our worship volunteers aren't validated in the ministry we lead, then they will undoubtedly look for another ministry where they are validated.

TEAM DISCUSSION QUESTIONS

- How can we make sure our culture is one of collaboration instead of command and control?

- In what ways are we regularly affirming our worship volunteers?

- What worship team policies should we have in place to outline clear and concise worship team expectations?

- How can we hold one another accountable to those expectations while still erring on the side of grace?

- How can we determine if our worship volunteers feel valued?

Chapter Thirty-One
Jump in the Deep End

Most worship conversations circle back to a binary discussion of hymns and modern worship songs only. Just considering those two worship options means we're satisfied with our congregation swimming in the shallow end of the pool. We must, instead, be willing to educate, enlighten, and coax them into the deep end.

Churches that won't take the risks to provide a venue for creatives to express art beyond predictable musical expressions will lose them to places that will. The emphasis on music as solely synonymous with worship may have actually hindered our worship and perpetuated conflict in our congregations. Considering additional artistic options could alleviate the pressure on music to serve as the primary driver of worship renewal and consequently diminish its solitary blame for worship conflict.

> In most traditions, music holds central place as, to use Martin Luther's term, "the handmaid of the Gospel." Whether Christians sing hymns, settings of the psalms, spiritual songs, anthems, or praise choruses, music is the principal artistic form that shapes Christian worship. But many others are involved. We gather in architectural structures; ... we listen to the literature of the Scriptures; we hear aesthetically crafted messages; we move in processions; and we view images ... associated with our faith. When we gather for worship art is all around us, and even within us.[1]

To go deeper we need to add the following to our worship vocabulary:

Worship is vertical, horizontal, meditative, reflective, sacrificial, celebrative, scriptural, prayerful, intergenerational, intercultural, global, local, personal, and corporate.

It's theological, visual, tactile, iconic, aural, verbal, instrumental, artistic, dramatic, aesthetic, imaginative, spontaneous, painted, danced, quoted, recited, sculpted, read, dressed up, dressed down, scripted, printed, and filmed.

It emotes through confession, invocation, supplication, intercession, meditation, celebration, lament, thanksgiving, anger, sadness, contemplation, joy, grief, despair, hope, pain, amazement, surprise, happiness, sorrow, shame, regret, hurt, peace, relief, satisfaction, fear, and love.

It remembers symbolically and sacramentally. Its prayers are both fixed and spontaneous.

It remembers the past, impacts the present, and challenges the future. It serves by doing justice, loving mercy, and walking humbly. It includes the Father, Son, and Holy Spirit. It gathers, exhorts, preaches, teaches, blesses, dismisses, and then sends out. It is continuous. And it also plays and sings psalms, hymns, and spiritual songs.

We tend to compare and contrast God's artistry based on our own musical history, practical experiences, and preferences. Limiting art to what we know and like assumes God only likes what we know. Depending on music as our only worship offering discounts God's calling for us to create and offer new art in response to diverse revelations. And since those callings are so unique to our contexts and cultures, how can our new art responses be contained in one expression?

Artistic worship beyond music is often seen as an extra offering meant for those who appreciate it and understand it but not for the rest of us. But we must all understand that art beyond music is, instead, an equally viable worship action essential to shaping our faith and worship understanding.[2]

Artistic balance is obviously necessary. For to insist that art is necessary for worship is to commit aesthetic heresy. Such insistence can make the expanded art understanding we are trying to encourage an idol or an object of our worship. But to insist art beyond music is a hindrance to worship is equally dangerous. It denies that material creation is a worthy vehicle through which God can communicate to us and we to God. Denying art in this role also denies the incarnation, for it was in human, material flesh that God became present to us in Jesus Christ.[3] To expand our worship vocabulary means that we, as worship leaders, are obligated to take the lead as mentors and shepherds. Our worship must freely and strongly say, "There is more, far more." Be hungry. Be thirsty. Be curious. Be unsatisfied. Go deep.[4]

TEAM DISCUSSION QUESTIONS

- How can we help our congregation go deeper in their worship understanding and expressions not only on Sunday but also during the week?

- What opportunities are we giving worship artists to express their art as worship beyond our traditional musical expressions?

- How can we introduce different worship expressions if our congregation is not accustomed to those expressions as acts of worship?

- What worship expressions might be inappropriate for the culture of our congregation and why?

Chapter Thirty-Two
Building a Wall

Senior adults are probably not as averse to worship change as they are to feeling marginalized through those changes. It seems to them that their opinions are no longer needed or considered and their convictions are discounted as antiquated. I can imagine that some seniors view change as something that separates what was from what will be. It appears that the price paid through their years of blood, sweat, tears, and tithes is now being used to build a wall that will sideline or keep them out completely.

Change is sometimes necessary when a church considers the culture and context of those present and those not yet present. But in an effort to initiate change, some congregations simply resolve to do anything different than what was done in the past.

They often change their worship styles and structures without ever evaluating their existing people and practices. That lack of planning and reflection can cause unnecessary transitional pain.

Defensive driving is operating a motor vehicle with an intentional awareness of your surroundings and the other drivers on the road. A defensive driver goes beyond the acceptable rules and basics of driving in order to reduce the risk of collisions. He or she plans ahead for the unexpected, anticipates adverse conditions, reacts to and respects other drivers, controls speed for quicker reaction time, and doesn't make assumptions about the intentions of the other drivers.

As a teenaged driver I learned the value of driving defensively when I was involved in a minor traffic accident. The elderly gentleman driving the other vehicle was ticketed for failing to yield to oncoming traffic, thus causing the collision. But when I walked over to ask if he was hurt, he responded with, "You were driving too fast." I was actually driving at a permissible rate of speed and obviously had the right of way; yet, he blamed me for the collision because I was going too fast *for him.*

In retrospect, I realize my inattentiveness didn't allow me to even notice his vehicle entering traffic from the side street until it nailed my right front fender. Even though this particular collision was not officially my fault, I wonder if it could have been avoided had I been driving more defensively? That's a great question for those of us who are worship leaders considering making radical changes. We are often just as inattentive as we move quickly from here to there without even considering our surroundings and others along the way.

Since change is often essential for churches to progress, the automatic assumption is that it will always require incorporating something completely new. It is possible, however, that the only thing necessary for congregational health and growth is to do what you are already doing... better.

Chip Heath and Dan Heath wrote, "We rarely ask the question: *What's working and how can we do more of it?* What we ask instead is more problem-focused: *What's broken and how do we fix it?*"[1] Maybe the change most of our congregations actually need is not a revolution but a reevaluation. A revolution forcibly overthrows an existing system or structure in order to substitute another. It replaces what presently exists without considering what might still hold value. In a revolution one side always loses. A reevaluation, however, examines something again. Reevaluation allows a congregation to consider change by rethinking, revisiting, and reinvestigating. Maybe a reevaluation instead of a revolution would allow us to tear down those walls between our generations.

Demolition, on the one hand, is the most expedient method of tearing down an existing structure in order to ensure that the ensuing structure bears no characteristics of the original. Does this sound like worship change in your congregation? In an effort to initiate worship change, leaders often use the finesse of a wrecking ball to swing wildly at existing practices. The consequence is often the complete destruction of the relational foundations of a community that may have taken decades to build.

Deconstruction, on the other hand, is the systematic and selective process of taking a structure apart while carefully preserving valuable elements for reuse. Deconstruction focuses on giving those valuable materials in an existing structure a new life. Healthier worship change is taking the time to recognize those components so they can be harvested and reclaimed as a foundation for useful building materials in the new structure. Craig Satterlee wrote, "Any change can be approached as either a threat or an opportunity, either a cause for celebration or a reason to despair."[2] Maybe our congregations will celebrate more often when our conversations begin with how we can prayerfully add to rather than arbitrarily take away.

TEAM DISCUSSION QUESTIONS

- How can we determine if the pace of our worship change is appropriate for multiple generations?

- What are we doing now that doesn't need to stop but needs to get better?

- What existing worship practices that do not seem to be working now can we deconstruct instead of demolish?

- How can we involve multiple generations in our worship change conversations without potentially jeopardizing the future of those changes?

Chapter Thirty-Three
Not Our Kind of People

Some of us can imagine our worship services filled with people of multiple colors, nationalities, economic levels, and political beliefs all worshipping God together. The only problem with that scenario is that most of us imagine how great that vision would be as long as those various cultures, tribes, and tongues are willing to adjust their worship to worship just like we do.

Early missionaries went to other countries and attempted to teach indigenous peoples to worship by singing western songs with western notation and western rhythms, only to realize that those indigenous people were not connecting with a deeper biblical and theological understanding of worship. It wasn't until the missionaries encouraged the use of native dance, tonalities, instruments, and rhythms that the various tribes were able to understand worship in spirit and truth. Why do we call it missions when we embrace cultural influences on worship internationally and call it compromise when we embrace those influences domestically?

"Not in my style" may really and truly mean "not my kind of people, except when it comes time for the yearly youth group trip to Mexico." We are willing to go outside the church to diversify but fail miserably to do so within.[1] So why are we so ready to defer when we travel around the world but not when we travel across town or even across the aisle?

In chapter 7 of Revelation, the multitude of God's people are standing before the throne of God. John's vision of every tribe and tongue worshipping together as one is a heavenly prophecy of intercultural worship. If we aren't meant to segregate by our cultures and generations as we worship in heaven, then why are we so divided as we worship here on earth?

- ## *We must stop trying to fix it with music.*

  We believe music is a universal language just as long as everyone else lives in our universe. It's impossible for intercultural worship to begin with a common musical style, so it must instead begin with a common biblical content. And when it does, music won't get the blame for what only theology can fix.

- ## *We must become ethnodoxologists.*

  Ethnodoxology encourages unity in the heart languages of those who are here and those who are not here yet. It looks beyond the assumption that Americans have a corner on worship understanding and considers the work that God is doing around the world and across town.

- ## *We must be mutually inconvenienced.*

  Mitch Albom wrote, "Sometimes when you sacrifice something precious, you're not really losing it. You're just passing it on to someone else."[2] Our worship success will be judged not solely on how well we did it ourselves but also on what conveniences we were willing to sacrifice so other people could do it too.

- ## *We must stop living monocultural lives.*

  Monoculture originated as an agricultural term that means the cultivation and growth of a single crop at a time. How can we expect to have intercultural worship on Sunday when we segregate monoculturally in everything else during the week?

- ## *We must have intercultural platforms.*

  Inserting the occasional international song is disingenuous when the people who lead those songs are homogenous. Harold Best wrote, "It is a spiritually connected culture that takes cultural differences, works through the tensions that they may create, and comes to the blessed condition of mixing and reconciling them and of stewarding their increase and growth."[3]

- *We must become uncomfortable with injustice.*

It is theologically incongruent to embrace cultural worship differences internationally while ignoring them domestically. American exceptionalism may be welcomed politically, but it can't be justified biblically. Worship that doesn't do justice by considering the voices of the marginalized is a worship God rejects.

TEAM DISCUSSION QUESTIONS

- Why is it that we are willing to make cultural adjustments when we do missions around the world but not when we are across the aisle?

- How can we create worship services that are welcoming to a variety of languages and cultures?

- In what ways can our worship move away from American exceptionalism without appearing to be unpatriotic?

- How can we transform our platform personnel to better represent the various cultures of those who are here and also those who are not here yet?

Chapter Thirty-Four
False Dichotomy

A false dichotomy is the belief that if one thing is true, then another thing can't be true. This comparison is typically used to force a selection between one thing or another by assuming that there are only two opposing positions. These either/or options are usually initiated to elevate one side over the other or to coerce participants to choose.

Even after a couple of decades, opposing or contrasting views are still being openly expressed and written about when it comes to hymns and modern worship songs. Those dialogues perpetuate either/or dichotomies by attempting to elevate one at the expense of the other. All-encompassing statements such as "modern worship songs are trite" or "hymns are archaic" continue to perpetuate the conflict. And those 7-11 monikers and old-time religion epithets that are neither funny nor accurate exacerbate the right/wrong and good/bad worship comparisons that are still dividing churches.

Defending one by criticizing the other is actually an act of self-defense, so it's usually preferential, not theological. Attempting to protect our favorite hymns or modern worship songs by vilifying the other can actually marginalize the one we are trying to protect. If they really need our feeble attempts to prop them up, then are they viable options? If, however, they can all stand on their own merit as many of us believe they can, then they will endure in spite of our criticisms and defenses.

As I write this, Major League Baseball is preparing again for a new season. Spring training is in full swing in Arizona and Florida. Thousands of minor league players are competing for a chance to prove their abilities at the major league level. Since its inception, Major League Baseball has had nearly twenty thousand players who've run up the dugout steps to play on a major league field. Approximately one thousand of those players have been called up from the minor leagues for just a single game. In baseball jargon, those players called up for a short time are referred to as "cup of coffee" players. The etymology of the idiom is that a player was only in the major leagues long enough to drink a cup of coffee before being sent back down to the minors. Most of the other roster players didn't have enough time to get to know them.

Congregations have literally hundreds of thousands of songs and hymns from which to choose to sing in their worship services. And since new songs are being written and added to the list every week, maybe the pressure to sing all of those new additions is actually causing congregational disharmony. Kenny Lamm wrote, "With the availability of so many new songs, we often become haphazard in our worship-planning, pulling songs from so many sources without reinforcing the songs and helping the congregation take them on as a regular expression of their worship."[1] So we aren't giving congregants the necessary time to resonate with and internalize new songs before we've moved to the next one.

The argument is not *if* we should sing new songs, since we have a biblical mandate to do so. The argument is *when* we sing new songs; let's give them enough time to become a part of our shared worship language. Let's call them up for more than a cup of coffee so we can all easily remember, revisit, and reaffirm their worship value for future services.

Modern worship songs and hymns and what follows them are here to stay. Instead of defending one by maligning the other, we should be praying that the peace of Christ would keep them and us in tune with one another. Additionally, we should be praying that our theological unity instead of stylistic aspersions would lead us to places way beyond our previous identities and imaginations.

Hymns and modern worship songs aren't mutually exclusive. As long as we are filtering them according to theology instead of partiality, they can both live in harmony and compatibility as worship allies instead of adversaries. When we do, we'll discover what it means to "glorify the God and Father of our Lord Jesus Christ together with one voice" (Rom 15:6).

TEAM DISCUSSION QUESTIONS

- How do we evaluate our song sets so they don't contribute to a false dichotomy of either modern songs or hymns?

- What process can we develop to continue teaching new songs while still retaining old ones?

- What evaluative processes should we use to determine if it is time to place a song on the shelf?

- Since regular attendance might only average a couple of Sundays a month, how often should we repeat new songs for them to become familiar to our church?

- How can we ensure that we are filtering our song selections according to theology instead of partiality?

Chapter Thirty-Five
Secret Worshipper

Most of us couldn't imagine leaving our children with a stranger in a daycare that has stained carpet, unpleasant odors, used toys, and old sound equipment stacked in the corner. But that is exactly what some churches offer to young parents and then wonder why they never return. The nursery and children's areas should be the safest and cleanest rooms in the building. So how can we expect parents to engage and understand meaningful worship at the same time they're worrying about the safety and health of their children?

My ministry responsibilities require me to travel pretty extensively. Because of the countless hours I spend driving the same roads, I'm familiar with the rest stops along those routes. I know the ones I'll stop at again because of their cleanliness and the ones I'll never return to because they're always filthy, never have the necessary supplies, and have archaic and often broken plumbing fixtures. We don't like to talk about restrooms at church, but that is the last place many worshippers visit before we ask them to join us in singing the first worship song.

Can you imagine a baseball announcer during the seventh-inning stretch encouraging the fans to turn around and greet one another after singing "Take Me Out to the Ballgame"? Or can you visualize an orchestra concertmaster asking you to find someone whom you don't know to shake hands with after the second movement of a Mahler symphony? How about asking worshippers to shake hands after the opening song at church? The worship service meet-and-greet can cause anxiety sweats and heart palpitations for first-time guests and congregational introverts. Many see that service element as shallow, contrived, and intimidating.

We are often good at considering our song sets and sermons but don't always consider worship distractions before, during, and after the worship services like those mentioned above. We often assume the theological depth of our worship will encourage visitors to return and maybe even stay. That possibility might actually be true if they could ever see past our logistical, spatial, and structural blind spots.

In addition to evaluating sermons and songs, churches should also evaluate their worship spaces and structures. We've all heard the adage about only getting one shot at a first impression. Since it's easy to overlook what we have gotten used to, it is helpful to secure an outside evaluator for a greater degree of unbiased and unprejudiced objectivity. Retailers, restaurants, and marketing firms often enlist casual outside patrons or shoppers to collect information about their establishment. They evaluate things like the appearance of displays, friendliness and efficiency of the staff, cleanliness of restrooms, or the prices and quality of their products.

Churches could also learn a lot about themselves by enlisting a secret worshipper. A friend from another congregation, an acquaintance from the community, or even your favorite coffee shop barista could be enlisted. For the minimal expense of a restaurant gift card you could invite one or several guests to visit your church and complete an evaluation questionnaire.[1]

Considering the above items and others might seem inconsequential compared to understanding spirit and truth worship. But guests often visit with little or no understanding of theological worship. They do, however, understand excellence, cleanliness, the safety of their children, and their own comfort. Isn't it worth the effort to remove some of those initial distractions that could be keeping them from going deeper?

TEAM DISCUSSION QUESTIONS

- How might we enlist someone from outside of our congregation to evaluate our worship?

- What worship practices have insiders become accustomed to that might be completely foreign to guests?

- How can we better evaluate what happens before and after the worship service that might be contributing to or distracting from worship health?

- How does our existing worship space contribute to or distract from worship?

Chapter Thirty-Six
Play the Ball Where
the Monkey Drops It

At the age of seventy-five, my father nearly died from West Nile Virus. His road back to health was rigorous as he spent more than one hundred days recovering in the hospital. Occupational and physical therapies were both necessary for a couple of years to combat the muscle weakness and paralysis from the virus that invaded his brain, causing swelling and permanent damage. The therapies allowed him to recover mentally, but the physical recovery eventually came to a stopping point. Consequently, he is no longer able to walk and is confined to a wheelchair at the age of eighty-nine. A resolve to make the best of his situation helped my father fight then and now to overcome and adapt with grace. Resilience allowed him still to live a productive, God-honoring life, even though it wasn't the life he would have chosen.

When facing difficulties in life, some of us are able to adapt and others get stuck or give up completely. Resilience is that ability to make adjustment when things don't go the way we hoped they would or planned. Those of us with resilience have the ability to amend our agendas, dreams, and desires by creating a new plan. Resilience doesn't mean we don't still feel the weight of our situation. It just means we look for available opportunities to make the best of it so we can continue to move forward.

Resilience is also a great characteristic for worship leaders to learn and develop. It encourages recovery with grace instead of overreaction in anger when the service doesn't go as intended. Resilience averts relational catastrophes when people don't react as we hoped they would react or when plans don't go as well as we prayed they would go. Even though worship leaders have the responsibility to prepare with excellence, they must also learn how to present with pliability, since the outcome of the service is not really theirs to control.

Thomas Merton wrote, "When humility delivers a man from attachment to his own works and his own reputation, he discovers that perfect joy is possible only when we have completely forgotten ourselves. And it is only when we pay no more attention to our own deeds and our own reputation and our own excellence that we are at last completely free to serve God in perfection for his sake alone."[1]

When the British colonized India they introduced the game of golf. After the first course was built in Calcutta, the monkeys in the surrounding trees would drop down, snag the golf balls from the fairways or roughs, and drop them in other locations. Golfers quickly learned that if they wanted to play on this course they couldn't always control the outcome of the game. Resilience finally helped the officials and golfers come up with a solution. They added a new rule to their golf games at this course in Calcutta: *play the ball where the monkey drops it.*[2]

None of us individually has enough creativity, insight, or endurance to plan, prepare, rehearse, and lead intergenerational, multisensory, and intercultural worship services in multiple styles week after week, year after year without making some mistakes. The psalmist wrote, "Sing to him a new song! Play your best with joyful shouts" (Ps 33:3)! We are indeed charged with playing and singing with skill and excellence. But excellence never means that we should leave relationships in our wake while moving toward the end result. The process with people is just as important as the destination.

The next time the organist and pianist begin playing a song in different keys, the next time the guitarist forgets to move his capo, the next time the tech team doesn't turn on your microphone or forward the text to the next slide, the next time the soprano section comes in too soon, the next time your bass player misses the first service because he forgot to set his alarm, or the next time your pastor cuts a well-rehearsed favorite song right before the service to provide more sermon time, just play the ball where the monkey drops it.

TEAM DISCUSSION QUESTIONS

- What is the difference between a culture of rigidness and one of resilience? Where does our team usually land?

- How do we encourage resilience without sliding into the acceptance of mediocrity?

- How is it possible to strive for excellence without leaving relationships in our wake?

- In what ways can we involve the entire team in evaluating a healthy balance of expecting excellence but also offering grace?

Chapter Thirty-Seven
Wasting Time

Our English language has only one word for time. But the ancient Greeks used two different words to distinguish between chronological time and theological time.

Chronos is sequential time that is orderly, rhythmic, and predictable. It is time that is externally controlled, can be measured by a clock, and is quantitative. Our words *chronological, chronic,* and *chronicle* are derivatives of this Greek word. *Kairos* is the time God chooses, not time measured or controlled by our clocks or us. It is time that could disrupt the normal flow of tradition, habits, methods, and ways of thinking. Kairos is qualitative and cannot be humanly manipulated or controlled.

We are sometimes guilty of trying to work up theological time or God moments in our worship services much like cheerleaders generate spirit at a game. Our actions can include a variety of scripted and synchronized routines such as songs, dances, chants, and stunts to rally enthusiasm, create energy, and spawn excitement.

But worship leaders are not cheerleaders, so they can't generate the spirit of God through their actions and song selections. Those actions might prompt, exhort, encourage, or even prod more response to the Spirit, but they can't work it up. As good as our various worship routines might be, they will never work up enough enthusiasm, energy, and emotion to create the Spirit that can only be recognized and responded to. We can acknowledge the Spirit, but we can't generate it. We can respond to the Spirit, but we can't initiate it.

The author of the book of Ecclesiastes understood kairos time when he wrote, "There's a season for everything and a time for every matter under the heavens: a time for giving birth and a time for dying, a time for planting and a time for uprooting what was planted, a time for killing and a time for healing, a time for tearing down and a time for building up, a time for crying and a time for laughing, a time for mourning and a time for dancing" (Eccl 3:1-4). The author continued with, "God has made everything fitting in its time" (Eccl 3:11). When Jesus's brothers fail to understand who he is, he tells them, for you, anytime is fine. But my time (kairos) hasn't come yet (John 7:6).

Kairos time is the moment of undetermined length in which the eternal (God's story) breaks into the temporal (my story), shattering and transforming it, and prepares the temporal to receive the eternal. It is the moment in which the conditional cancels itself out and makes itself the instrument of the unconditional.[1]

In a chronos approach to worship, a congregation asks God to enter its story or the story of its own making. In a kairos approach, the congregation is asked to enter God's story. Kairos might occur in the former but has already occurred in the latter.

So here is a question we should ask as we plan and lead worship each week: "Are we missing kairos moments in our efforts to manufacture creative worship services?" If we are, then we may be placing more focus on the creative than the creator. God has provided Scripture, prayer, and the Lord's Supper as kairos opportunities for us to join God's story. In our creativity and innovation are we minimizing God's time (kairos) in order to give more time (chronos) to other service elements of our own making?

TEAM DISCUSSION QUESTIONS

- Are there any recent examples where it seemed like we became cheerleaders instead of worship leaders?

- How often are we guilty of placing more focus on the creative than on the creator?

- What kairos worship elements have we minimized in order to elevate our chronos worship elements?

- Can our worship generate or initiate the presence of the spirit of God or just acknowledge and respond to it?

Chapter Thirty-Eight
Cheap Worship

When Jesus engaged the Samaritan woman at the well, the conversation moved from the physical (thirst) to the spiritual (living water). She attempted to change the subject back to the physical of the *where and how* of worship, but Jesus turned the conversation again to her spiritual condition and the *who* of worship: "God is spirit, and it is necessary to worship God in spirit and truth" (John 4:24).

Once the woman encountered and acknowledged Jesus, she joined his conversation instead of expecting him to join hers. This divine encounter inspired her to sacrifice the self-serving agenda that originally brought her to that place. She *left her water pot* and went into the city and said to the people, "Come and see a man who has told me everything I've done! Could this man be the Christ?" (John 4:29).

The result of the Samaritan woman's worship response was, "Many Samaritans in that city believed in Jesus because of the woman's word when she testified, 'He told me everything I've ever done'" (John 4:39).

In the book of Romans, Paul focused on the divisions by which we segregate ourselves. In the twelfth chapter he wrote, "So, brothers and sisters, because of God's mercies, I encourage you to present your bodies as a living sacrifice that is holy and pleasing to God. This is your appropriate priestly service" (Rom 12:1). Sacrifice is surrendering for the sake of something or someone. It is the act of giving up, offering up, or letting go. A baseball bunt is a sacrifice for the sole purpose of advancing another runner. Executing this sacrifice is called *laying down* a bunt.

We go to great lengths and personal expense to make sure our children and grandchildren have the best clothes, schools, lessons, and coaches. We begin economizing and genericizing the moment they are born in order to save money and set it aside for the best of college educations. We surrender our own personal wants, preferences, and even needs so that they will have everything necessary for a successful future. In fact, most of us would literally give our own lives for our children and grandchildren because no sacrifice is too great—except maybe when we're asked to sacrifice our worship music preferences.

Sacrificing our preferences often requires us to adjust generationally and relationally. Terry York and David Bolin wrote, "We have forgotten that what worship *costs* is more important than how worship *comforts* us or how it *serves* our agendas. If worship costs us nothing but is fashioned to comfort our needs and preferences, it may not be worship at all."[1]

TEAM DISCUSSION QUESTIONS

- What are we as worship leaders willing to sacrifice as our spiritual act of worship?

- How might the way we select and lead songs be contributing to an attitude of worship comfort instead of cost?

- How can we make sure we are not asking the same generations or cultures always to be the ones who sacrifice the most?

- How do we keep the cultural attitude of entitlement out of our worship services?

Chapter Thirty-Nine
We're Talking about Practice

Worship that continues after we leave the Sunday service is always easier when things seem to be going our way. It's easy to worship when we have a job we love, when our family is healthy, when we're living in our dream home with a stable family, and when our finances are secure. But what about when the daily circumstances of life overwhelm us? Worship is our response to God's revelation in the past and God's continuous revelation in the present. God's revelation is perpetual, meaning it doesn't start and stop according to the various circumstances of life. So, consequently, our responses shouldn't either.

In an often-replayed press conference, basketball superstar Allen Iverson responded to questions from reporters about his team, the Philadelphia 76ers, losing to the Boston Celtics in the first round of the playoffs. When asked if the focus of a closed-door discussion with his coach Larry Brown occurred in response to his habit of missing practice, Iverson responded: "Hey, I hear you, but we're talking about practice, man. We're not even talking about the game, when it actually matters, we're talking about practice." Iverson repeated the word *practice* twenty-two times.

A reporter followed up with this great question, "Is it possible that if you practiced you could help make your teammates better?" Iverson responded with, "How in the (expletive) could I make my teammates better by practicing?"

In the seventeenth century, at the age of twenty-four, Lawrence of the Resurrection, born Nicolas Herman, joined the Discalced Carmelite order

102

of the Catholic Church in Paris. Brother Lawrence was an uneducated monk serving as a cook in a French monastery. The recorded words in his journal reflect his understanding of practicing the presence of God when he wrote, "The time of action does not with me differ from the time of prayer; and in the noise and clutter of my kitchen, while several persons are at the same time calling for different things, I possess God in as great tranquility as if I were upon my knees at the Blessed Sacrament."[1]

Practice is repeated performance or systematic exercise for the purpose of acquiring skill or proficiency. It is learning through repetition, which then becomes habit. Brother Lawrence wrote, "There is not in the world a kind of life more sweet and delightful, than that of a continual conversation with God; those only can comprehend it who practice and experience it."[2] He was not frustrated with his manual labor. In fact, he found himself in God's presence while peeling potatoes as well as when he was kneeling in prayer.[3]

If worshippers habitually practiced the presence of God throughout the week, then what could occur when they got to practice God's presence together on Sunday? Although our verbal response to practicing the presence of God during the week may not be as overtly profane as that of Allen Iverson, our actions often convey the same disdain. We aren't practicing God's presence when we think our times of prayer are different from other times because we are as strictly obliged to cleave to God by action in the time of action as by prayer in the season of prayer.[4]

Our singular focus on Sunday worship may be communicating that worship begins and ends with our opening and closing songs. Is it possible that if we practiced worship during the week we could get better and also help make our teammates better? Continuous worship stems from lives of continued prayer since worship is an ongoing conversation with the one who lives within us.[5] When we understand that kind of practice, then what occurs on Sunday will be an overflow of what has already occurred during the week with the added benefit of getting to then practice it with others.

TEAM DISCUSSION QUESTIONS

- How are we modeling practicing the presence of God during the week?

- What are some indicators that we are placing too much emphasis on Sunday worship at the expense of worship during the week?

- What would Sunday worship look like if it were an overflow of a congregation practicing the presence of God?

- How will we actually know when our congregation has embraced an attitude of practicing worship as a continual conversation with God?

Chapter Forty
Worship Karaoke

Karaoke singers are provided with a microphone, sound system, and projected text for the purpose of imitating a familiar song originally recorded by a popular artist. They are judged on how well (or poorly) they imitate the original artist.

Karaoke happens in churches every Sunday as they try to imitate other congregations or artists without considering the culture and context of their own congregation or its leaders, players, and singers. Worship karaoke is no respecter of styles so it can appear in the form of a choir in tuxedos, sequined dresses, and coiffed hair; or a band in jeans, shirttails, and unkempt hair.

It is often easier to imitate the worship habits, methods, styles, presentations, and even attire of other artists or congregations. We sometimes mimic them without even considering our own gifts and calling or the calling and abilities of our players, singers, and congregants. Then we are often disappointed when those players and singers don't live up to those unreal expectations.

If God has entrusted us with our position, then imitating or mimicking the worship of another congregation actually marginalizes that calling. An imitation can never exceed the quality or ability of the imitated or it is no longer an imitation but instead a new creation. An imitation will always be an inferior substitute for the original. Is that really what God intended for us and the best we have to offer him and his church?

Obviously, not all congregations are gifted with musicians who can create original songs and therefore must borrow their songs from others. The difference between borrowing and imitating, however, is taking the time to interpret those songs for your own congregation. Instead of imitating the worship style of other congregations, we should be trying to discover our own unique worship voice.[1] Finding the voice of a congregation is not just following a recipe or imitating the success of other artists and congregations. The voice of your congregation "is found by listening to its overtones. It is the voice heard and shared when the congregation prays together, eats together, cries and rejoices together. It is the voice heard and shared when a congregation works out its differences, blesses its children, buries its saints, and sings its carols of love and hope."[2]

Shared events impact the formation of a congregation's worship DNA. That unique worship voice is shaped while suffering through the moral failure of a leader, while walking in the grief of a catastrophic tragedy, while trying to survive a church split, during the communal rebuilding process of a storm-damaged facility, or when encountering exponential growth. Can a congregation ever worship the same during or beyond the occurrence of one of those events? Just imitating the worship voice of another congregation marginalizes those shared experiences for both congregations.

Imitation is about style. Interpretation is about content. Imitation is based on replication. Interpretation is based on revelation. Imitation ignores God's limitless creativity in multiple contexts. Interpretation acknowledges God's limitless creativity in your own context. Imitation is an attempt to lead worship by mimicking what someone else has been called to do. Interpretation is an attempt to lead worship by expressing what God has called you to do. Worship leaders, if the only version of worship songs we ever lead or our congregation ever expects are exactly like the original artist's (including genre, key, tempo, instrumentation, vocal timbre, volume, attitude, and attire), then why do they need us?

TEAM DISCUSSION QUESTIONS

- What worship methods, habits, or styles are we presently implementing in our services just because we saw they were successful somewhere else?

- How are we intentionally discovering the creative abilities of those not yet in our worship ministry?

- In what ways can we borrow the worship practices of other congregations while still considering the culture of our own congregation?

- What are some of those shared events that have helped form the worship DNA of our church?

Chapter Forty-One
Stop Singing

Our worship actions can drown out the distinct voice of God that is often only discernible in the silence. In the midst of our self-generated noise, we can miss healing, comforting, and encouraging words of hope such as "I am with you," "Well done," "You are forgiven," and "I am weeping with you." Scripture is certainly not silent on silence: "That's enough! Now know that I am God!" (Ps 46:10). "Don't be quick with your mouth or say anything hastily before God, because God is in heaven, but you are on earth. Therefore, let your words be few" (Eccl 5:2). There's "a time for keeping silent and a time for speaking" (Eccl 3:7).

Gary Furr and Milburn Price wrote, "In the drama of the Christian life, worship may be thought of as the script through which the Author of us all calls forth and responds to the deepest and most important longings in us."[1] Until we stop to listen, how will we hear that call?

A rest is a musical notation that indicates the absence of sound but not the end of music. John Ruskin, a Victorian-era English art critic, said this of the silence of music and rests:

> There is no music in a rest, but there is the making of music in it. In our whole life-melody the music is broken off here and there by rests, and we foolishly think we have come to the end of the tune. God sends a time of forced leisure, sickness, disappointed plans, frustrated efforts and makes a sudden pause in the choral hymn of our lives, and we lament that our voices must be silent, and our part missing in the music which ever goes up to the ear of the Creator. Not without design does God write the music of our lives. But be it ours to learn the tune, and not be dismayed at the rests. They are not to be slurred over nor to be omitted, nor to destroy the melody, nor to change the keynote. If we look up,

God Himself will beat the time for us. With the eye on Him, we shall strike the next note full and clear.[2]

Musical rests add depth and emotion to a musical score through the use of silence. They both create and relieve tension. They allow the players and singers to take a breath before the next difficult musical passage. Rests create a deliberate pause or temporary break in the action and keep the notes from being strung together in breathless chaos. Playing music without rests is like driving a car without brakes.

Worship is a conversation that requires not only speaking and singing but also hearing and listening. The noise of our sermons and songs as our only act of worship can create monological worship. Our offering of one-sided worship sound can monopolize the conversation, potentially causing us to miss the voice of God. The foundation of meaningful worship is instead dialogical. It is an interactive exchange of two or more participants. Healthy conversations include a balance of discussion and response, listening as well as speaking. Since God began the conversation and graciously invited us to join in it, our worship could then be enhanced and renewed when we stop trying to monopolize the conversation with our responsive noise only.

We rely on the words of our sermons and songs to manage and control others. A frantic stream flows from us in an attempt to straighten others out. We want so desperately for them to agree with us, to see and sing things our way. We evaluate, judge, condemn, and devour congregants with our words. Silence—as one of the deepest spiritual disciplines—puts a stop to that.[3]

To again hear and listen to God's side of the conversation, maybe it's time to concur with Samuel in our services of worship, "Speak, Lord. Your servant is listening" (1 Sam 3:9).

TEAM DISCUSSION QUESTIONS

- How can we incorporate silence as a part of our services when it hasn't been part of our worship culture?

- What are we presently doing that is contributing to worship noise?

- How is our worship encouraging our congregation to not only hear but also listen?

- What can we do differently to give time for the various worship elements to breathe without interrupting our worship flow?

Chapter Forty-Two
Awful Worship

awful [aw–fuh'l]—1. solemnly impressive; exceedingly great; inspiring awe.
2. full of awe; reverential.[1]

Awe is the act of worship in response to the mystery of God. It causes us to respond with, "Mourn for me; I'm ruined! I'm a man with unclean lips, and I live among a people with unclean lips. Yet I've seen the king, the LORD of heavenly forces" (Isa 6:5). Moses understood awful worship when he was instructed to take off his sandals because he was on holy ground, causing him to hide his face because he was afraid to look at God (Exod 3:5-6).

God is transcendent, both unknown and unknowable. He is beyond, above, other than, and distinct from all. Isaiah prophesied, "My plans aren't your plans, nor are your ways my ways, says the LORD. Just as the heavens are higher than the earth, so are my ways higher than your ways, and my plans than your plans" (Isa 55:8-9). Consequently, a faith such as ours rooted in the infinite cannot be contained in our finite understanding. The paradox, however, is that this transcendent, unknown, and unknowable God is constantly revealing himself to us and seeking our worship. The unknown seeks to be known and acknowledged. There is certainly something awful about that.

Our culture, however, has responded by demanding the reduction of God's mystery to something we can explain. We have transformed our response to the awe, mystery, and transcendence of God into a scheduled event. When we take surprise out of worship, we are left with dry and dead religion; when we take away mystery, we are left with frozen or petrified dogma; when we script awe, we are left with an impotent deity; and when we abandon astonishment, we are left with meaningless piety.[2]

109

A. W. Tozer wrote, "We cover our deep ignorance with words, but we are ashamed to wonder, we are afraid to whisper 'mystery.'"[3] But then Scripture again reminds us of his mystery, "God's riches, wisdom, and knowledge are so deep! They are as mysterious as his judgments, and they are as hard to track as his paths! *Who has known the Lord's mind? Or who has been his mentor? Or who has given him a gift and has been paid back by him?* All things are from him and through him and for him. May the glory be to him forever. Amen" (Rom 11:33-36).

My doctoral thesis advisor wrote, "The teacups of our thinking and language have not yet approached the capacity of holding the ocean of divine truth."[4]

Mystery is not just our limited capacity to understand and explain the entirety of God's story; it is also the incomprehensible awe and wonder at being included in that story. Can that ever be scripted? If the awe and wonder of God can be contained in and explained in our limited understanding and expressions of worship, then he is a god who does not deserve that worship.

Michael Yaconelli wrote, "The critical issue today is dullness. We have lost our astonishment."[5] He continues by stating, "The greatest enemy of Christianity may be people who say they believe in Jesus but who are no longer astonished and amazed. Jesus Christ came to rescue us from listlessness as well as lostness; He came to save us from flat souls as well as corrupted souls."[6]

Contemplating the depth of God must include the mystery of God creating, the mystery of God incarnate, the mystery of the cross and empty tomb, the mystery of God's presence in the church, and the mystery of Christ's return to claim lordship over creation.[7] If the gravity of that mystery doesn't continually inspire us with awful, wide-eyed wonder then no songs we select ever will.

Changed from glory into glory,

till in heav'n we take our place,

till we cast our crowns before Thee,

lost in wonder, love and praise.[8]

TEAM DISCUSSION QUESTIONS

- How is it evident in our sermons and songs that we aren't comfortable with mystery?

- How do we keep from scripting awe out of our worship?

- When was the last time our congregation was lost in wonder, love, and praise?

- What should we be doing differently to make sure our worship services are well planned while still leaving room to be surprised by God?

TEAM DISCUSSION QUESTIONS

How is worship like an usher ministry? Why is that comparable and appropriate?

How do we keep from making worship a performance?

When have you seen worship done well? How and why was it done well?

What should we be doing differently to address this issue? What actions could we take in how worship is to be implemented by us?

Chapter Forty-Three
Not the Bride

Most Protestant churches have rejected the old covenant practice of recognizing priests as a special class of religious hierarchy. Even though some congregations have retained the title, their priestly function is often a pastoral role as ministers rather than as interceders. The belief that someone else must mediate our relationship with God for us or dispense God's grace to us was set aside through the foundational doctrine of the priesthood of every believer.

If worship leadership is always done by a select few, then we may be continuing to feed that priestly misconception. Those who lead worship should instead take on that responsibility like an usher in a wedding. The duty of a wedding usher is to help others find their place in the wedding ceremony. They accomplish this task without coercion or force by offering their arm as an encouragement for participants to accompany them.

Ushers always move at an appropriate pace as they guide and exhort friends and family to their proper locations. It is often necessary for ushers to arrive early and stay late since they have just as much responsibility before and after the ceremony as during it. And the best ushers are those who are friendly, genuine, and welcoming without needing to be acknowledged, honored, or credited.

Even though ushers play a key role in the wedding ceremony, they must have enough humility to acknowledge they aren't and won't ever be the bride. Leading worship like an usher with an attitude of humility is one of the most difficult qualities for a worship leader to embrace and sustain. In the name of a higher calling we are often unwilling to take a secondary and supportive role.

Scripture offers Jesus as "a priest in the holy place, which is the true meeting tent that God, not any human being, set up" (Heb 8:2). In this place of ministry, Jesus became our liturgist and serves as our mediator. As the tabernacle and its elements are described, the author of Hebrews points out that the old covenant limited access to God. Only the high priest was allowed into the holy of holies one time a year with a blood offering (Heb 9:3, 6-7). The place where God's presence was most realized was not available except through the high priest and only at certain times of the year.

In the new covenant, however, Jesus became the mediator and serves as the intercessor for the people of God. An earthly priest was no longer required; the sacrifice was complete; Jesus's blood was offered; the veil was torn in half; and the way was now open for all to worship God without an earthly mediator. Most churches embrace that shift theologically and doctrinally but sometimes continue to function with leaders who are still serving as earthly high priests.

Worship leaders' calling is to invest in, not intercede for, our congregations. That responsibility is Jesus's alone, not ours. The death and resurrection of Jesus reminds us that all may enter into the presence of God with boldness not available in the restrictions of the old covenant. Our responsibility is to serve our congregations like an usher by exhorting them to an understanding that "we have confidence that we can enter the holy of holies by means of Jesus' blood, through a new and living way that he opened up for us through the curtain, which is his body, and we have a great high priest over God's house" (Heb 10:19-21).

TEAM DISCUSSION QUESTIONS

- How might our worship leadership habits be causing us to appear as the bride instead of an usher?

- What would leading like an usher look like each Sunday in the worship culture of our congregation?

- How can we hold one another accountable if we are to start moving toward leading worship on behalf of instead of with our congregation?

- If we only have a limited pool of qualified worship leaders, then how do we keep from giving the impression that worship can only be led by a select few?

Chapter Forty-Four
Crossing the Rubicon

Instead of fulfilling the Great Commission by tapping into the unlimited creativity available from the creator, some of us continue trying to reach the culture by offering a mediocre musical imitation of what that culture already has. We play it safe by impersonating the language, structure, dress, and music, usually a few notches below in quality or a few steps after culture has moved on to something new. Offering a weak impersonation of the practices of a culture that doesn't know what it needs to try to reach a culture that doesn't know what it needs can't be the best we have to offer. Maybe it's time for our churches to cross the Rubicon.

In 49 BCE, Julius Caesar led a single legion of troops across the Rubicon river on the way to Rome. This bold move was considered an act of insurrection, since Roman generals were prohibited from bringing troops into the home territory of the Republic. If Caesar and his men failed to triumph, they would all be executed. Caesar and his men determined that this point of no return was worth the risk. Their boldness ultimately protected Rome from civil war and also ensured the punishment for their actions would never be necessary.[1] The idiom "crossing the Rubicon" now refers to an individual or group willing to radically commit to a revolutionary and sometimes-risky course of action when playing it safe will no longer suffice.

When king David and his men brought the ark of the covenant back to Jerusalem, he was so focused on responding to God's blessings that he danced right out of his robes. With complete disregard for previous worship practices or what others might think, David danced with all his strength in complete humility before the Lord (2 Sam 6:14).

David's wife and Saul's daughter, Michal, was not nearly as enthusiastic about his new worship practices. In fact, Scripture says, "Michal was watching from a window. She saw King David jumping and dancing before the Lord, and she lost all respect for him" (2 Sam 6:16). Michal's traditionalism caused her to miss participating in a profound response to God's revelation. Her primary focus was on how David worshipped.

David admonished Michal that it wasn't for her or her father that he danced. Instead, he was celebrating before the Lord, who chose him over her father and his entire family (2 Sam 6:21). His primary focus was on why he worshipped. He was willing to cross the Rubicon because of *the why* even though it meant changing *the how*.

Crossing the Rubicon should never cause a church to compromise biblically, theologically, or doctrinally but will often require it to make worship adjustments in order to accommodate culturally, contextually, and systematically. The conviction to fulfill the Great Commission and the collaboration to do it together are the unifying factors that inspire leaders and congregants to go all in and refuse to retreat. A unified commitment can give us all the resolve to cross the Rubicon even when the end result is uncertain.

Leaving here to cross over there means churches can't continue to dance to the same tune of what they prefer. They can't stay here when they are called to go there, even when here is more certain and comfortable. It will certainly require entrepreneurial innovation instead of routinized imitation, or becoming artisans instead of assembly-line workers. But being willing to cross that Rubicon may also then mean that our churches will "speak to and among the surrounding culture in a voice so unique, authentic, and unified that it turns heads: 'what was that? It sounded like nothing I've ever heard before. I've never heard anything like that around here.' Even though those responses from the culture will often come as ridicule, they might just as often come as inquiry. Either way…the church will be influencing culture instead of just reflecting it."[2]

TEAM DISCUSSION QUESTIONS

- How might our worship look different if we tried to impact the culture instead of just imitating it?

- What is the worship Rubicon our church needs to cross but hasn't because of the fear of conflict?

- How can we know when it's time to actually cross our Rubicon?

- What processes might help us mitigate the inevitable pain of leaving here when we are called to move there?

Chapter Forty-Five
Missing the In-Between

Having unified worship in a culture of generational differences requires biblical understanding, prayer, sensitivity, discernment, and sacrifice. Fusing congregants immersed in a postmodern world with those still longing for the comforts and familiarity of a modern world usually increases the divide. One generation wants to continue having "do you remember" conversations while the other longs for "can you imagine" conversations. Conflict seems inevitable as both worlds attempt to find worship common ground.

Since the membership of most congregations includes a cross-section of individuals from both worlds, which world do we choose when planning and implementing worship?

The longing for what *was* of one generation and the hope for what *could be* of another generation may be causing both to miss worship in the *in-between*. Sometimes we are so focused on the past or the future that we miss the present.

Anthropologist Arnold van Gennep identified and examined patterns of transition and renewal within communal systems. In his study, van Gennep referred to this season of social transition as the *rites of passage*. As a living organism, a community of faith passes through developmental transitions as a natural progression of the life of that congregation and as a reflection of the surrounding culture.[1]

Victor Turner continued van Gennep's study by refining an understanding of the rites of passage as a time of separation from what was known to a transitional or *liminal stage* that would ultimately lead to a reaggregation or reincorporation.[2] The word *liminal* originated from the Latin word *limins*, meaning threshold.[3]

In his book on worship transformation, Timothy Carson wrote, "Liminal reality is that space and time that has broken with prevailing structure, whatever that may be. Precisely because it is positioned between the structures of life, it holds latent power for future transformation."[4]

Liminality is the place where we find ourselves in our present culture of worship. Ironically, it can be a time of unity in our shared uncertainty. One of the shared struggles of this stage is determining how to balance the desires of some for complete abandonment of previous worship practices with the desires of others to hold on to those foundational touchstones. In-between is not wasted time. It's not just preparation. It is not throwaway time. And it's not a warm-up for what is to come. Liminality reminds us that the worship journey is as important as the worship destination.

My family loves to vacation in the mountains of Colorado in the summer. One summer several years ago, we made plans ahead to climb one of the fifty-three mountain fourteeners. In the mountaineering vernacular, a fourteener is a mountain peak with an elevation of at least fourteen thousand feet. Climbing at that altitude for flatlanders is a pretty daunting task. Our ultimate goal was to reach the summit. But what I hadn't realized is how meaningful the trip up to the summit would be.

We passed fields of snow even though it was the middle of July. We came upon an old abandoned mineshaft. We traversed narrow trails through the trees but then stepped out to the open expanse above the tree line around twelve thousand feet. We also passed other climbers coming down from the summit who offered encouragement while we continued to suck air. The journey was difficult, but reaching the summit wouldn't have been nearly as fulfilling if we hadn't gone through it together as a family.

Balancing generational and cultural worship predilections will be realized when a congregation understands how to embrace transformation as formative rather than rejecting it because of hesitancy to change. Although that liminal stage can be a time of uncertainty, it can also be a time of hope, expectation, and even unity. While we are trying to figure it out, we are trying to figure it out *together*.

Turner referred to a special camaraderie that can often develop among those sharing a liminal stage as *communitas*.[5] The spirit expressed in this Latin noun is the harmony within a community based on its common purpose, not necessarily on its common practices. Encouraging a spirit of *communitas* enables those who are sharing a liminal stage to develop a community of the in-between. This relationship "creates a community of anti-structure whose bond continues even after the liminal period is concluded."[6]

117

Ultimately, worship reaggregation is indeed necessary for a healthy balance. But it may take much longer if both worlds don't figure out how to get along in that in-between. If we can't figure out how to get along on the journey, then how can we expect to get along once we arrive?

TEAM DISCUSSION QUESTIONS

- How can we encourage more "can you imagine" conversations while still respecting those "do you remember" conversations?

- Are there any recent examples of us being so focused on the end result that we missed worship in the in-between?

- Does our Sunday worship encourage an attitude of *communitas*? Is that organic or planned?

- How can we make sure our congregation always feels like they are part of figuring things out together?

Chapter Forty-Six
Letter to the Younger Me

Dear Younger Worship-Leading Me,

In a few decades you are going to look back at your years of worship ministry with a desire for a second chance to handle some things differently. You will think about certain services, special events, entire seasons of ministry, or strained relationships and long for another opportunity to make some adjustments.

The reality is that it will be impossible for you to go back and make corrections to most of those situations. But with a little humility, resilience, and resolve now, you have an opportunity to get some of them right the first time. So here are a few things you are going to learn.

Surround yourself with those people who will stretch your thinking and actions but also hold you accountable. Taking necessary risks might cause you to make some mistakes, but the discernment of others will help protect you from your own stupidity. It might be exhilarating when you succeed alone, but it won't be when you fail alone. And you will sometimes fail.

People will always remember how you treat them when you're off the platform more than how you lead them on the platform, so learn more people's names than new songs. Consider their interruptions as divine appointments instead of distractions. Drink more coffee with senior adults and ask their opinions before initiating change. Be more patient with needy people and chronic takers. And remember to thank those who make sacrifices to invest in you, your family, and your ministry.

Be on the front end of learning new musical and technological languages. But don't assume it's always appropriate to be an early adopter of them. Being conversant in a language doesn't mean it should be used when it doesn't fit

119

the voice of your congregation. Learn more theology than musicology, and practice leadership development more than you practice your guitar.

Always ask how something might impact your family before asking how it might impact your worship-leading. Leave more things at the office when you go home, and be home when you are home. Taking a Sabbath each week will not only help your spiritual and physical health but also help the relational health of your family.

Stay longer instead of bailing for a new place of ministry every couple of years. If your ministry frequently moves your children away from their friends and foundations, then how can you expect them to like church when they are no longer required to attend?

What you know about worship-leading now won't be enough to sustain you through your entire ministry. Read more, study more, and ask more questions. Be a lifelong learner who understands it's never too soon or too late to learn something new.

Finally, I know it is sometimes overwhelming to balance the stresses of ministry and family. When leading worship is discouraging, when it seems like no generation is ever completely happy, when you can't sing too many or too few hymns, and when you wake up on Monday morning and wonder if this is really worth it, you can rest assured that you'll also be able to look back at those decades of ministry and acknowledge with certainty that it was worth it.

TEAM DISCUSSION QUESTIONS

- What worship-leading situation or relationship failure that occurred in the past would we handle differently if we had the chance?

- What safeguards could we put in place to make sure the same situation doesn't occur again?

- How successful are we at stretching one another's thinking and holding one another accountable?

- With our limited time together to get ready for Sunday, how can we continue to learn new worship principles and practices in addition to new songs?

Chapter Forty-Seven
Send in a Canary

Taking a canary into a coal mine served as a warning system in the earlier days of mining. Canaries are sensitive to methane gas and carbon monoxide, making them ideal for detecting a dangerous buildup of gas in the subsurface mines. The canaries would begin to show signs of distress in response to small concentrations of gas before it became detrimental to the miners. The first sign of imminent danger was when the *canary stopped singing*. The idiom continues to refer to a person or thing that serves as a warning of a looming crisis.

If certain generations, cultures, or even the majority of your congregants have stopped singing, it is a warning sign of danger ahead. Intentionally asking questions not only about the singing of our congregation but also about the way we are leading that singing could alert us to a potential conflict while there is still time for restorative care.

Elevated volume levels could be contributing to the decline in congregational participation. Being sensitive to the need for minor sound adjustments could encourage expanded participation. Kenny Lamm wrote, "If our music is too loud for people to hear each other singing, it is too loud."[1] We often get caught up in our world of musical production and lose sight of our purpose to help the congregation voice their worship. Let them know you expect them to sing by finding the right balance—strong, but not overbearing.[2]

We all know volume complaints are more prevalent when the complainant doesn't particularly like the musical style. So sending in a canary to evaluate the volume of your singing is not a stylistic issue. An organ, choir and orchestra, rhythm section, or southern gospel quartet all have the same potential to hover around elevated or even damaging volume levels. In fact, some studies have shown that incidents of hearing loss are slightly higher in classical musicians than rock musicians. So even if our volume preferences may be subjective, the potential effects are not.

Worship leaders often use the Occupational Safety and Health Administration (OSHA) decibel scale to determine acceptable levels. Although a helpful resource, it is often used reactively rather than proactively. In other words, leaders use this scale to defend existing levels in response to complaints. Proactive use of the OSHA scale can instead help a congregation consider not only acceptable levels but also appropriate levels. Acceptable levels are subjective. Appropriate levels are objective. Slight volume adjustments could foster significant progress toward more appropriate worship music to encourage active participators instead of passive spectators.

As leaders, we rationalize higher decibel levels because it feels better, because it fits a certain genre, or because we just prefer it at those levels. And yet, we often vilify congregants who make those same claims about their own preferences. It's really just a matter of our responsibility and accountability as leaders to fulfill our obligation to steward the congregants we have been entrusted to lead.

Adopting an early warning system is a preemptive process of enlisting congregational canaries before it is too late. It is vital to enlist those who love God, love the church, and love you enough to honestly evaluate your leadership and assess the level of congregational participation. The humility necessary to initiate this process and the willingness to sacrifice your own interests for the good of your church can only occur if you also love God, love the church, and love the people enough to trust their assessment.

TEAM DISCUSSION QUESTIONS

- What processes could we use to evaluate whether our congregation is singing or just watching us sing?

- How do we determine an appropriate decibel level for our congregation?

- How does our congregation know when they are expected to sing and when it is time to listen?

- What additional hindrances could be contributing to a decline in congregational participation through singing?

Chapter Forty-Eight
Stick the Landing

Ageism has impacted most of us serving in worship leadership. Churches seem to be on the lookout for a younger platform presence or fresher image from those who lead. Forced termination or demotion as a result of the ageism epidemic reminds us that where we serve is not always ours to control. What we can control, however, is that we are prepared to continue to serve somewhere. What if what we once learned is not enough to sustain us through our entire ministry? What can we do that will allow us to continue?

A gymnastic competition can be won or lost in the landing. Even if you flip, vault, tuck, and twist well during the routine, it isn't a success unless you also stick the landing. Halftime is over, and some of us are well into the last quarter of our worship-leading career. We've accumulated decades of knowledge, experience, and practical application so we know how to work smarter. But just working smarter isn't helping some of us finish well. How can we stay viable, battle ageism, and keep from coasting in order to stick the landing?

- *Learn a new language.*

    Even though we might be fluent in previous worship languages, we also need to learn the musical and technological vernacular of newer worship languages and what might follow them. When we lose the resolve to learn, we lose the resolve to lead. It's never too soon or too late to learn something new. The end of learning new is the beginning of leading old.

- *Force quit.*

    Computer programs sometimes become unresponsive. Selecting force quit reboots and reinstates the original well-functioning settings. Quitting

123

doesn't mean we stop doing worship ministry or have to leave our present position. It just means rebooting for a fresh start where we are now.

- ### *Extend your shelf life.*

Shelf life is the length of time items are given before they are unsuitable for use. It is the time in which the defined quality remains fresh, acceptable, viable, usable, and effective under normal circumstances. Increasing our shelf life encourages us to recalibrate or fine-tune for the potential of a new reality.

- ### *Get another job.*

Agreeing that worship leader ageism is unjust or theologically suspect doesn't change its reality. We can choose to live in a constant state of fear in the last quarter, or we can proactively prepare in case ageism does occur. Learning additional marketable skills doesn't compromise our calling; it actually enhances that calling beyond choirs and chord charts. Retooling could help us stick the landing where we are now or maybe where God will call us next.

Some of us enjoy running, cycling, or other exercises to help us extend our shelf life physically and to relieve stress as we age. A few years ago, I ran the Kansas City Marathon with my daughter. Leg cramps at mile twenty-one seemed to seize up every muscle in my legs. Marathon runners call this "hitting the wall" or "bonking." If I hadn't trained and fueled properly before the race, I would not have been able to complete it. After massaging those muscles and walking some I was able to continue the race with the help of my daughter's encouragement. Even though my time was not as good as I had hoped it would be, I was still able to cross the finish line.

Distance runners have to push themselves beyond their level of comfort to log the miles necessary to compete. If they haven't done the roadwork ahead of time, the minute the pace quickens, the incline increases, or the terrain gets treacherous, they will be tempted to quit.

Many of the stressors of ministry have little to do with our lack of skill but instead result from a lack of preparation. Scripture challenges us to stick the landing this way: "No discipline is fun while it lasts, but it seems painful at the time. Later, however, it yields the peaceful fruit of righteousness for those who have been trained by it. So strengthen your drooping hands and weak knees! Make straight paths for your feet so that if any part is lame, it will be healed rather than injured more seriously" (Heb 12:11-13).

TEAM DISCUSSION QUESTIONS

- What are some valid reasons a church might replace a worship team member?

- How can we help aging worship team members continue to learn newer musical and technological languages?

- How can we help worship team members retool for other ministries when they are preparing to step aside from worship leadership?

- What accountability guidelines do we have to help one another run this race with endurance?

Chapter Forty-Nine
More Than a Memorial

A limited understanding of the Lord's Supper only as a penitential replay of the Last Supper may have diminished its significance for our churches. This traditional approach is not inaccurate, just incomplete. Considering the Lord's Supper as more than a memorial allows us to remember not only what Christ did for us in his death and burial, but also what he continues to do for us through his resurrection and promised return. The visual, tactile, and symbolic Word of the Table should cause us to grieve that his body was broken for us. The remembrance is not just to live in the past through our sorrow but also to remember in order to influence our present and future.

As shown in the book of Acts, the early church frequently celebrated the Lord's Supper, not just as a memorial of the crucifixion but also as a celebration of the resurrection. Remembrance or *anamnesis*, according to Jewish understanding, was not merely mental recollection of the actual repetition of the event. Instead, *anamnesis* was a celebration of the past event in order to live in its experience and participate in its redemptive qualities each and every time.[1]

Considering the Lord's Supper beyond a memorial is an adjustment of our attitude not just at the Table but also in what we sing, the text we read, and our words of instruction. Songs and Scripture focused on the cross are obviously valuable for expressing our worship at the Table. But songs and texts focusing on the horizontal communal relationship with each other and thanksgiving that we get to be a part of the story can be equally valuable.

COMMUNION

Congregations are constantly looking for ways to connect with one another in community through affinity and spiritual relationships. An attempt to create or re-create this affinity through our musical selections alone is often a shallow attempt to manufacture what is already available in the communion found at the Table. Communion is defined as an act of sharing and is never a solitary act. Paul speaks of communion as the fellowship of sharing in the body and blood of Christ. He affirmed this when he stated, "Isn't the cup of blessing that we bless a sharing in the blood of Christ? Isn't the loaf of bread that we break a sharing in the body of Christ? Since there is one loaf of bread, we who are many are one body, because we all share the one loaf of bread" (1 Cor 10:16-17). Leonard Vander Zee wrote, "The Lord's Supper not only gathers a community, it creates a community."[2]

Two relationships are evident in this communal celebration: a vertical obedience and communion with Christ through partaking of the elements and the horizontal fellowship of believers unified in identity and relationship at the Table. The Lord's Supper is not only a time of personal assessment but also a time of corporate evaluation. The process of self and congregational appraisal encourages unity and, as a result of that unity, intimacy that cannot be manufactured.

A biblical understanding of how Communion creates community is offered in the example of the two disciples in Luke 24 who recognized Jesus in the breaking of the bread. Henri Nouwen points out that Christ living in them brought them together in a new way. The breaking of the bread allowed them to recognize not only Christ but also each other as members of the new community of faith.[3] Nouwen wrote, "Communion makes us look at each other and speak to each other, not about the latest news, but about him who walked with us."[4]

EUCHARIST

In some church cultures *Eucharist* is a liturgical term or observance we either have never heard of, won't consider because we don't understand it, view as something mystical, or won't implement because it seems too "Catholic." The word *Eucharist* originated from the Greek word for thanksgiving, gladness, or blessing. It is recorded in the book of Acts: "Every day, they met together in the temple and ate in their homes. They shared food with gladness and simplicity. They praised God and demonstrated God's goodness to everyone" (Acts 2:46-47).

The Eucharist helps us understand that remembering is not just to live in the *past* through our sorrow but also to remember in order to influence our *present* and *future.* It allows worshippers to move from symbolically wallowing in the sorrow that their sin caused Christ to die, to realizing that thanksgiving is found in the resurrection and his ultimate return. Experiencing joy at the Table does not diminish the sorrow of the cross and sinful nature of the world. In fact, just the opposite occurs as it reminds us that even in the midst of misery, hope is available. With that understanding, how can we keep from offering our thanks?

The challenge for those of us from church cultures that have not observed the Lord's Table in this way is not to disregard these understandings out of fear that expanding our observances will take our congregation to a doctrinal place it has never been before. Instead, we should prayerfully consider the attention that must be given to this ordinance each time it is observed so that worship renewal found at the Table is never a one-time event. Robert Webber said it this way, "The idea is very simple: when we remember the death (Lord's Supper), celebrate the resurrection (break bread), and eat a meal expressing covenantal relationship with God (Communion), we need to give thanks (Eucharist)."[5]

TEAM DISCUSSION QUESTIONS

- Why do we celebrate the Lord's Supper in exactly the same way every time we observe it?

- What does Scripture say about how often and in what ways we are to observe the Lord's Supper?

- How might we sing differently if we celebrated the Lord's Supper not just as a memorial of the Last Supper but with an attitude of thanksgiving in response to the resurrection?

- What is the difference, if any, between Communion and the Lord's Supper?

- How could our congregation respond to celebrating the Lord's Supper eucharistically within the parameters of our doctrine?

Chapter Fifty
Give Me a Break!

More than a decade ago a store called MinneNAPolis opened in Minnesota's Mall of America. It rented spots for tired shoppers to take power naps or get away from the stress of the mall. The new store included rooms such as Asian Mist, Tropical Isle, and Deep Space. The walls were thick enough to offer quiet relief from the sounds of the mall outside. Guests could listen to music, take a nap, enjoy a massage, or just remove themselves for a few minutes from the hectic atmosphere of the mall. All of this was available for only seventy cents a minute. It seems like fourteen dollars for twenty minutes of napping would actually cause more stress.

Sunday isn't a day of rest for those with worship-leading responsibilities. Some are probably wondering whether they have enough in the tank to do it all again next week. If Sunday isn't their Sabbath, when is? Most worship team players and singers are volunteers with full-time jobs outside of their worship-leading responsibilities. They don't have the freedom to take off the Monday after or the Friday before Sunday like some of those in full-time ministry do. If we don't establish a regular rotation of players and singers to allow them to catch their breath, then how can we expect them to lead others to a place they no longer have the spiritual, emotional, or physical resolve to go to themselves?

Jesus said, "Come to me, all you who are struggling hard and carrying heavy loads, and I will give you rest. Put on my yoke, and learn from me. I'm gentle and humble. And you will find rest for yourselves. My yoke is easy to bear, and my burden light" (Matt 11:28-30). Offering regular rhythms of rest for our worship teams means we are helping one another remove those self-made yokes. The word *rest* in this passage is better translated as refreshment. As a college student I worked a couple of summers installing aluminum siding, screen rooms, and even an aluminum swimming pool enclosure. The pool enclosure was installed around and over a preexisting pool that was full of water. Screws driven into the structure with powered screw guns held the aluminum joists and panels together. Inevitably, some of the screws fell into the pool. So it was my job to dive into the pool several times each day to retrieve those screws so they wouldn't clog the pool filter and pump system. I certainly understood that word *refreshment* in the middle of a workday in the summer heat. That rest or refreshment didn't relieve me of my work responsibilities; it just provided a time of respite in the midst of them.

Refresh means to renew, revive, or reinvigorate. Refreshment is not idleness; it isn't an exemption; and it's not laziness or a free pass. It is instead an intentionally deep-calming physical and spiritual peace. Isaiah also spoke of this kind of rest: "Don't you know? Haven't you heard? The LORD is the everlasting God, the creator of the ends of the earth. He doesn't grow tired or weary. His understanding is beyond human reach, giving power to the tired and reviving the exhausted. Youths will become tired and weary, young men will certainly stumble; but those who hope in the LORD will renew their strength; they will fly up on wings like eagles; they will run and not be tired; they will walk and not be weary" (Isa 40:28-31).

Jesus didn't challenge us to do something he was not practicing himself. He said, "Put on my yoke, and learn from me" (Matt 11:29). After feeding the five thousand, he perceived that the crowd would try to come and take him by force to make him king. The text says Jesus took refuge *again*, alone on the mountain (John 6:15). The word *again* indicated he had been there before. After John the Baptist was beheaded, Jesus encouraged the disciples who had been working very hard and were grieving to "come by yourselves to a secluded place and rest for a while" (Mark 6:31).

It is evident in chapter 12 of Matthew that Jesus is Lord of the Sabbath, and we aren't. Chapter 11 ends with him reminding us to take his yoke because it is easy and his burden is light (Matt 11:29-30). A good yoke fits the necks of the oxen. Its edges are polished smooth and rounded. When a yoke fits perfectly, the oxen can haul heavy loads every day for years. This text is a great reminder for us to lead worship with margins of recovery by bearing his yoke instead of those stressful burdens of our own making.

TEAM DISCUSSION QUESTIONS

- If Sunday is not the Sabbath for us because of our many worship-leading responsibilities, then when is?

- How can we possibly hold one another accountable when we are worn out?

- What processes have we put in place to give team members a break?

- How can we expect to lead others to a place that we no longer have the resolve to go to ourselves?

- How can we know if we have taken Jesus's yoke instead of a yoke of our own making?

Chapter Fifty-One
It's Not an Experience

Marketing is an intentional process of identifying who the consumer is, determining the wants and needs of that consumer, and offering a product that satisfies those wants and needs in order to secure their loyalty.

Marketers have realized that consumers no longer just want to buy a product; they also want to buy an experience with that product. In fact, sometimes the experience is much better than the product. Think about some of those pizza arcades where you celebrated your children's birthday. Fortunately the experience was memorable; the pizza certainly wasn't. Instead of just purchasing a cup of coffee, many of us also now want *the experience* of purchasing a cup of coffee. We are even willing to pay extra for the sights, sounds, and smells of that experience. It's an added bonus to that experience when the barista knows your name.

Social media has contributed to an experiential consumerism marketing culture in which our posting experience is enhanced by the number of likes, shares, retweets, or comments. Those of us who are social media aficionados have learned how to market our posts to encourage a more favorable experience. Some of us plan and lead worship the same way.

In an effort to entice more participation, churches offer worship service preferential experiences to get consumers in the door, sometimes even at the expense of quality or honesty. These marketing headlines attract visitors with words such as *traditional, contemporary, blended, friendly, family, fellowship, multisensory, relevant, modern, casual, classic,* or even *coffee.* But when guests realize worship is something you give, not something you get, how will we encourage them to stay? If we market just by catering to experiential tastes, what will we offer when their tastes change?

We can experience a fine meal. We can experience a baseball game, concert, or amusement park. An experience is an event or occurrence. We even call what we do on Sunday a worship experience. But an experience is something that is done to us or for us. Worship is something we do.

We don't experience worship: we experience God. Our response to that experience is worship. We can experience the many facets of God inside or outside a worship service, but the experience or encounter is not worship—our response is. A worship service built on an experience alone is incomplete if it never allows us an opportunity to respond.

Depending on worship as an experience can cause us to be satisfied with the sensations elicited by that experience. Consequently, we might select and sing certain songs or even styles of songs because of the experience and then never move beyond that experience to worship. Again, as with social media posts, there is a danger that we might select our songs and sermons in response to positive, negative, or no feedback. And if those songs and sermons don't create and re-create that same experience each week, we can leave a worship service believing worship couldn't and didn't occur.

TEAM DISCUSSION QUESTIONS

- How can we offer creative worship opportunities without our services deteriorating into experiential consumerism?

- What is the difference between experiencing worship and experiencing God?

- How can we demonstrate to our congregation the difference between God's revelation and our response?

Chapter Fifty-Two
Playing Hurt

Shake it off. Take one for the team. These are adages we often hear from sports coaches and fans. Publicly acknowledging injuries can sideline players and even threaten their future with the team. Players often play through their pain, knowing that it's often easier for a team to replace rather than rehabilitate them. This same pattern of expendability is also evident in a church-worship culture. Worship leaders often sense a profound pressure to perform even when they might not feel like it. To secure their positions, they often play hurt.

Serving in worship leadership doesn't mean you are immune from the personal struggles of life, such as depression, anxiety, physical health issues, marital conflict, or financial strain. Most congregations don't fully realize the physical, emotional, mental, and spiritual demands required for someone to serve as a leader of worship. Individuals are often aware of the investments their worship leaders have made in their own life and the lives of their family members. What they don't often calculate, however, is the cumulative time and energy those investments require when multiplied by the entire membership population of a congregation.

Worship leaders are often seen as personal counselors, mentors, leaders, friends, and spiritual advisors. When families are in crisis, those worship leaders are expected to referee, repair, and reclaim. At the same time, they are required to challenge their congregation to respond to God's revelation with stellar worship every Sunday. If all congregants have the same expectation that their worship leaders will willingly respond to their every need, then how can we not expect the stress of that responsibility to eventually take its toll? Safeguards aren't often put in place to help worship personnel. Congregations find it easier just to replace them.

Free solo climbing or *free soloing* is climbing without safety ropes, harnesses, protective gear, or the assistance of other climbers. The free soloist relies only on his or her own strength, ability, and mental determination. Most of us can't imagine taking the personal risk required to participate in such an extreme sport as free solo climbing. And yet, we continually lead our ministries and organizations while depending only on our own strength, ability, and talent. As a result, the personal risk and the risk to our worship ministry could be just as catastrophic.

Physical and mental stamina alone can't protect the free soloist from loose rocks or sudden changes in weather. The dangers associated with this form of extreme climbing cannot be controlled completely by the abilities of the climber. When a mistake is made or outside forces intervene, free solo climbers rarely get a second chance.

The term *belaying* refers to a variety of techniques used in climbing to exert friction on a climbing rope so that a falling climber does not fall very far. A belayer is a climbing partner who secures the lead climber at the end of a rope and belays out rope as needed. When a lead climber loses his or her footing, the belayer secures the rope, allowing the climber to regain a secure foothold to continue the climb.

The reality is that many of us in worship leadership are so talented that we can fake it and succeed alone for a time. The reality is also that our talent will only take us so far, and the time will come when the inherent risks of free soloing will cause us to fall alone. If your congregation is not willing to put a safeguard in place to invest in your physical, emotional, mental, and spiritual health as worship leaders, then maybe it is time to consider another congregation. The author of the book of Ecclesiastes said it a little more tactfully: "Two are better than one because they have a good return for their hard work. If either should fall, one can pick up the other. But how miserable are those who fall and don't have a companion to help them up! Also, if two lie down together, they can stay warm. But how can anyone stay warm alone? Also, one can be overpowered, but two together can put up resistance. A three-ply cord doesn't easily snap" (Eccl 4:9-12).

TEAM DISCUSSION QUESTIONS

- Why have churches created a culture that requires its worship leaders to fake it when they are wrestling with some of the normal struggles of life?

- What processes should we put in place to rehabilitate leaders instead of replacing them?

- How will we know if someone is ready to serve again?

- How might the worship of our congregation be sincerer if worship leaders could openly model worshipping through pain?

- If we haven't put safeguards in place to offer physical, emotional, and spiritual healing and hope for our worship leaders, then who will?

Conclusion

Instead of evaluating worship health based on biblical foundations, theological tenets, and historical precedents, churches often attempt to heal their worship by randomly adjusting their song selections, radically changing their worship styles, and hiring or firing worship staff. Diagnosis is the process of determining by examination and evaluation the nature and circumstances of a diseased condition. Treatment is the administration and application of remedies once the diagnosis has been determined. We seem to continually invert these two processes when considering worship renewal.

Intentionally evaluating before indiscriminately implementing can provide a constructive process for a congregation to verbalize foundational worship principles. Once those deeper biblical and theological principles are solidified, congregations can then set treatment goals for their worship practices. Trial-and-error treatment focused on style and service mechanics will continue to consume the energy of worship planners and leaders unless an organized diagnostic plan is put in place. The result is often worship unhealthiness that is much more contagious. But if we ensure our diagnosis always precedes the treatment, our worship renewal prognosis can't help but offer more hope and health.

The primary worship leader can't accomplish comprehensive worship evaluations in his or her own power. If the structure and content of our worship service is always determined by the evaluations of the same person or even a select few, then our worship reality is limited to our own assumptions. Those ideological assumptions can blind us to worship that may not actually be occurring. Involving our congregation in evaluating our worship is only possible if we have enough humility to admit we love God and the church more than we love unfettered control. Outsourcing some of those responsibilities means we will encourage worship freedom instead of control.

Control is conditional or contingent on something or someone else. It relies on or requires the aid of another. Worship control is saving it until Sunday and waiting for someone else to initiate it. It focuses only on what is done for us here and has to start over every week. It increases worship conflict since we only get one chance at it.

Conversely, freedom increases permission for our congregations to make choices and to transform those choices into worship responses not only when they gather but also when they leave. Worship freedom equips and offers encouragement to think, behave, or take action autonomously. Freedom can reduce conflict since we all get multiple chances at it. It then leads to the full, conscious, active, and continuous participation of all worshippers.

When worshippers are given freedom and are no longer controlled in their worship preparations, presentations, and evaluations, what was once a weekly gathering will become a daily occurrence. Then we won't just draw the blinds while we wait for Sunday. We will all be constantly in touch with the work God is actually doing and know how to respond to it the moment it occurs.[1]

Appendix One
Worship Evaluation Questionnaire

Unless an organized plan of evaluating worship based on the deeper biblical and theological issues is implemented, style and service mechanics will continue to consume the energy of worship planners and leaders. An intentional evaluation process would provide "a constructive way to articulate what a congregation has learned about itself and its worship practices, as well as to prioritize which goals are most important to address in the future."[1]

Since most congregations do not have an instrument to regularly evaluate their worship, the following questionnaire was developed to encourage those congregations to consider worship renewal grounded in Scripture and modeled throughout the history of the church. Worship evaluation *will* occur. Leaders must determine if they would rather initiate the evaluation or constantly respond to congregational critics who have initiated the evaluation for them. A preemptive approach could reduce the conflict that will inevitably occur from the latter.

WORSHIP EVALUATION QUESTIONNAIRE

*Service Date:*_____ *Service Time:*_____

ENTRANCE/GATHERING

When were worshippers first greeted after leaving their cars?

Observations:

Was an attitude of community evident as the congregation gathered?

Observations:

Were worshippers embraced as a part of this community during the gathering?

Observations:

Was the congregation publicly invited to participate in this worship service?
Examples: invocation, hymn/song, call to worship, and processional.

Observations:

CONGREGATIONAL SINGING/PRESENTATIONAL MUSIC

Was the congregational singing passive or participative?

Observations:

Did the music selected for congregational singing include a balance of familiar
and new?

Observations:

Did congregational song selections include vertical, horizontal, celebrative, and
reflective expressions?

Observations:

Did presentational music encourage congregational participation or passivity of
performer and audience?

Observations:

Was the text of the music theologically sound, and did it affirm the Scripture as central?

Observations:

Was the music intergenerational and culturally appropriate for this congregation?

Observations:

Did music get too much attention in this service?

Observations:

VISUAL AND FINE ARTS

Were visual and/or fine arts incorporated into this service? Examples: mime, drama, dance, poetry, painting, sculpture, video, or film.

Observations:

Did the use of the arts in this service contribute to or distract from the worship expressions?

Observations:

Was it evident through these arts that worship is visual as well as verbal?

Observations:

Were artistic expressions used inappropriately in this worship service? Examples: glory of man instead of God, manipulation, or entertainment.

Observations:

PRAYER

Was it evident that prayer was an important part of this worship service?

Observations:

Who led in prayer? What types of prayer were led? Examples: invocation, confession, supplication, intercession, communion, lament, thanksgiving, or repentance.

Observations:

Were prayers fixed and/or spontaneous?

Observations:

Were various prayer postures encouraged?

Observations:

SCRIPTURE/SERMON

In this worship service was it evident that Scripture is foundational?

Observations:

What Scripture passages were read in this service?

Observations:

Who read Scripture? How was it read?

Observations:

Was Scripture read beyond the text for the sermon?

Observations:

Was there a sense that the sermon came after the "preliminaries," or was it evident that the sermon was a part of the worship?

Observations:

Did the congregation actively participate in the reading of Scripture?

Observations:

ORDINANCES—LORD'S SUPPER/COMMUNION/ EUCHARIST/BAPTISM

Was Communion celebrated in this service? If so, what was the attitude of the observance? Examples: communion, thanksgiving, remembrance, celebration, or eschatology.

Observations:

Did the Lord's Supper provide an opportunity for symbolism and mystery?

Observations:

Was the Lord's Supper central to the worship theme of this service?

Observations:

If the Lord's Supper was not celebrated, what other options were available for responding to the Word? Examples: offering, congregational singing, baptism, testimonies, prayers of confession, invitation, Scripture, or presentational music.

Observations:

Was baptism celebrated in this service? Did the baptism contribute to the communal relationship of the congregation?

Observations:

Was the symbolism of baptism evident and understood by members and guests?

Observations:

DISMISSAL

How was the congregation dismissed at the end of the service?

Observations:

Was the dismissal a sacred expression? Examples: blessing, challenge, communal action, or recessional.

Observations:

Was there a communal and unified attitude evident as the congregation left?

Observations:

ADDITIONAL ELEMENTS

Where were the announcements presented? Did they distract from the flow of worship?

Observations:

Was the offering a time of sacrificial response that encouraged an attitude of worship?

Observations:

What additional elements were present in this service?

Observations:

GENERAL WORSHIP ELEMENTS

Did the service feature a balance of worship actions? Examples: praise, confession, dedication, commitment, response, or lament.

Observations:

Was the service conversational, involving God's words to us and our words to God?

Observations:

Did the worship space encourage my participation in worship? Examples: icons, art, symbols, colors, or lights.

Observations:

Was the order of service easy to follow or confusing?

Observations:

Did the service flow well? Did transitions link the worship elements? Was the pace satisfactory?

Observations:

Did the worship leaders convey a genuine pastoral concern?

Observations:

Which of the five senses were employed?

Observations:

Was there a good balance of celebration and contemplation?

Observations:

Were there elements of the service presented by leaders that could have been presented by the people? Examples: prayer, Scripture reading, or testimonies.

Observations:

Were physical actions encouraged? Examples: raising hands, kneeling, bowing head, palms upturned, clapping, or standing.

Observations:

Did the service give participants an opportunity to connect with one another?

Observations:

What symbols were used in this worship service?

Observations:

Did anything in the service distract my attention from a conversation with God?

Observations:

Were guests able to meaningfully follow the service without confusion? Were elements presented that were generally accepted by the congregation but that might be unfamiliar to a guest? Were these elements explained?

Observations:

Did the service offer a time of silence for reflection, repentance, or confession?

Observations:

Besides congregational singing, what elements offered an opportunity for active participation?

Observations:

Did the worship service invite the congregation to be a part of God's story through Jesus Christ?

Observations:

Appendix Two
Lord's Supper/ Communion/Eucharist Questionnaire

To assist in understanding the value of the Lord's Supper to worship in our congregation, please answer the following questions based on your perspective as a worship planner/leader/congregational participant. Please answer the questions thoroughly with regard to current understanding and practice, not future aspirations.

Name (optional):

1. How important is the Lord's Supper to our congregation?

2. How often is the Lord's Supper included as a part of our worship services? How is this determined or scheduled?

3. What is the attitude of our congregation during the Lord's Supper, and what determines that attitude?

4. What does the Lord's Supper signify to you personally? What factors contribute to this significance?

5. Do you believe the Lord's Supper has worship value for you individually? If yes, in what ways? If no, why?

6. Do you believe the Lord's Supper has worship value for our entire congregation? If yes, in what ways? If no, why?

7. Have you observed or participated in a Lord's Supper service in a congregation or denomination outside of ours? If yes, give a brief explanation.

8. Were any of those experiences particularly meaningful for you? If yes, please list examples and reasons why.

9. Were any of those experiences uncomfortable for you or confusing to you? If yes, please list examples and reasons why.

10. Could any observances of the Lord's Supper listed in response to question 7 enhance the worship of our congregation? If yes, please give examples of how.

11. Is the Lord's Supper central to the worship theme of our services? If yes, how? If no, why?

12. Does our Lord's Supper theme vary from observance to observance? If no, why? If yes, what elements contribute to those various observances? Examples: remembrance, communion, or thanksgiving.

13. Does the observance of the Lord's Supper in our church strengthen your relationship with God? If yes, what elements contribute to that? If no, what elements distract from that?

14. What could/should be done differently that would enhance the Lord's Supper services in our church?

15. Any additional comments?

Appendix Three
Secret Worshipper Questionnaire

Our goal in enlisting you as a Secret Worshipper for _____
Church is to help us learn how to better welcome first-time guests and embrace them as a part of our church family. We want to be a church that people not only want to visit the first time but also want to return to again because of their initial experience. For that to occur we know we must strive to get better each Sunday.

The reason we have enlisted you is that we want unbiased and objective feedback about things you observe that we are doing well and areas in which we need to improve. We know how easy it is for us to overlook those things we have gotten used to that will be more obvious to an outside observer. As you respond to these questions, please be completely candid and as thorough as possible. We have included questions for you to consider before, during, and after the service. We know we are sometimes better at thinking about the things during the service and can forget those distractions before and after the service. Thank you for helping us surface those areas we are missing so we can overcome our blind spots and be a place where people of all generations and cultures want to connect.

SECRET WORSHIPPER QUESTIONNAIRE

Was it easy to get into the parking lot and convenient to park?

Observations:

Was it clear where you were supposed to go once you arrived?

Observations:

Was the property in good repair and grounds well kept?

Observations:

When were you first greeted, if ever?

Observations:

Did the attitude of the greeter make you feel welcome?

Observations:

Were you offered coffee, and was it excellent, mediocre, or bad?

Observations:

Were the foyer colors and decorations outdated?

Observations:

Did it seem like people were happy to be there and glad to be together?

Observations:

Were the handouts timely and of excellent quality?

Observations:

Was the restroom clean and odor free?

Observations:

Did you feel comfortable leaving your child in the children's ministry area?

Observations:

Was the worship space interesting and pleasing to the eye?

Observations:

How did you figure out where to sit?

Observations:

Did you feel conspicuous when you entered the worship space?

Observations:

Was the worship center seating comfortable?

Observations:

Was there enough light?

Observations:

Was the temperature at a comfortable level?

Observations:

Did anyone dress or look like you?

Observations:

How was the volume of the speaking and music?

Observations:

Did the leaders use language you didn't understand?

Observations:

How was the service flow and pace?

Observations:

Did the service seem too long?

Observations:

Was the worship service order easy to follow or confusing?

Observations:

Was it easy to participate musically?

Observations:

Was the music presented with excellence?
Observations:

Was the music culturally relevant for the people present?
Observations:

Were the video projection elements presented with excellence?
Observations:

Did you feel welcome to participate in all worship service elements?
Observations:

Was the sermon easy to follow and meaningful?
Observations:

Did any of the service elements make you feel uncomfortable?
Observations:

Did anything in the service distract you?
Observations:

How did you know what to do when the worship service was over?
Observations:

Did anyone speak to you after the service?
Observations:

Were the members friendly, unfriendly, or disinterested?
Observations:

Did the leaders seem approachable?
Observations:

Any additional observations?
Observations:

Would you come back based on your observations?
Observations:

Worship Leader/Worship Team Relational Contract

A relational contract is a voluntary agreement between two or more parties that clarifies the expectations of their association in order to diminish conflict, encourage unity, inspire trust, and foster mutual accountability. What if worship leaders and worship teams planned, prepared, and presented worship with a relational contractual agreement as one of the foundational components of their leadership? Can you imagine the worship health potential this could offer your congregation? Unfortunately, this type of worship-leading relationship rarely occurs because leaders often function as independent contractors reliant on their own strength, ability, methods, processes, and talent.

Implementing a relational contract will require a level of sacrifice and trust that is not guarded, territorial, defensive, or competitive. It could serve as a useful guide to hold one another accountable to the unified goal of fulfilling the mission of your church. But it will obviously never occur unless and until all parties are willing to embrace it. In an effort to more effectively lead, exhort, teach, and model healthy worship, we as the primary worship leaders agree to adhere to the following relational guiding principles. We understand that the worship of our congregation will never be completely healthy until our relationship as its leaders is also healthy.

_____, *Worship Leader*

_____, *Worship Team Member*

_____, *Worship Team Member*

_____, *Worship Team Member*

_____, *Worship Team Member*

_____, *Worship Team Member*

We agree that we will:

- Maintain a collaborative spirit that supports all of our worship gifts as complementary, not competitive.

- Publicly and privately acknowledge the value of our unique callings, leadership styles, gifts, and competencies.

- Listen as often as we speak.

- Partner in leading and teaching worship that moves beyond musical style alone to deeper biblical and theological content.

- Communicate our disagreements in private without fear of retribution.

- Make every effort to be approachable, available, and accountable to one another.

- Affirm in public; correct, instruct, coach, and mentor in private; and pastor one another at all times.

- Sacrifice individually for the sake of the body corporately.

- Initiate intentional significant conversations that include our hopes, dreams, goals, expectations, plans, concerns, and evaluations.

- Invest in the personal and spiritual development of one another with no ulterior motive.

- Preserve loyalty, trust, morality, respect, and friendship.

- Work toward a common philosophy of worship and ministry.

- Pray consistently for and with one another.

Internal Evaluation Framework

Evaluating worship from the inside is an internal process of enlisting individuals and groups from within your congregation to regularly evaluate present worship structures and practices. Inside or internal evaluators already understand the culture, doctrines, and personnel assets or liabilities that frame your worship preparation and implementation. They have a vested interest in the process and results since it is their church too.

Internal evaluation is a valuable instrument once a framework for a deeper understanding of worship renewal has been established and practiced. The danger of internal evaluation without a deeper understanding is the perpetuation of ideological evaluation based on likes and dislikes, mechanics and styles. The benefits, however, outweigh the risk of encountering the occasional ideologue.

INTERNAL EVALUATION RECOMMENDATIONS

- Develop an evaluative team for worship-planning and follow-up evaluation. Include musicians, theologians, technicians, artists, and so on.

- Video the platform personnel (including the pastor) as an evaluative tool for the team. Look for: genuineness, preparedness, idiosyncrasies, platform presence, vocal clarity, language clarity, and so on.

- Video the congregation before, during, and after worship services to evaluate how or if they are participating.

- Enlist intergenerational and intercultural congregants to respond to questions regarding the relevance of worship to their generations or cultures.

- Ask evaluation team members to sit in various places during worship services to consider volume, balance, pace, flow, content, congregational participation, and so on.

- Enlist nonmusicians to respond to musical questions.

- Ask an educator to evaluate language and grammar usage of platform leaders.

- Encourage nontechnical congregants to respond to projection, sound, lighting, and other technical/logistical questions.

- Implement platform personnel peer-to-peer evaluations.

- Keep it simple. Don't attempt to evaluate too much at a time.

- Design evaluations to minimize the focus on style and personal preferences. Avoid questions that elicit "I like" or "I don't like" answers.

- Ensure evaluations aren't used to manipulate or provide justification for biases.

- Evaluate strengths as well as weaknesses.

Appendix Six

Congregational Suggestions for the Language of Lament

The language of lament is found in more than half of the psalms but is largely absent in much of the Protestant culture. Lament is that healthy, open expression of pain, complaint, sorrow, anger, frustration, and grief directed at a God who understands. If congregations are to experience renewal of the biblical understanding of lament and its appropriateness in their worship culture, they must consider how to implement this communal response as a regular part of their liturgy. The following list is not an exhaustive one but is a place to begin the conversation.

- ### *Leaders must model lament.*

  Modeling will require leaders not just to preach, teach, and sing about the psalms of lament but also to live them with their congregation. In response, congregants must allow their leaders the freedom to express their own vulnerabilities without fear of reprisal. When leaders introduce lament to a worshipping community through the articulation of common experience, the sorrow worshippers and leaders share validates those expressions.

- ### *Read all of the Psalms.*

  It is ironic that our worship culture so rabidly defends the Word as foundational to our faith and practice, yet limits its use only to palatable text that does not offend. John Witvliet reminds us that "when faced with an utter loss of words and an oversupply of volatile emotions, we best rely not on our own stuttering speech, but on the reliable and profoundly relevant laments of the Hebrew Scriptures."[1]

- ### *Pray the Psalms.*

A meaningful approach is to pray a lament psalm corporately in response to a specific lamentable situation. Psalm-praying gives voice to the timid and unity to the lamenting body. Praying psalms of lament can take us deeper much quicker than we are often able or comfortable going on our own. Eugene Peterson, in *Answering God*, reminds us that, "left to ourselves, we will pray to some god who speaks what we like hearing, or to the part of God we manage to understand. But what is critical is that we speak to the God who speaks to us. . . . The Psalms train us in that conversation."[2]

- ### *Incorporate lament beyond contrition.*

If we have participated at all in lament in our public and private worship practices, it has likely been as a response to sorrow and despair over our sinful nature. We are often more comfortable with contrition, since we can admit that our struggle is something we caused and there is no one to blame but ourselves. This alleviates our discomfort and fear of the appearance of faithlessness by questioning God in our lament language. Contrition in response to our sinful nature is indeed a necessity. But we must also admit that lament in response to circumstances beyond our control is also necessary.

- ### *Sing songs of lament.*

Until recently, the writers and composers of hymns and modern worship songs were not publishing many songs to help a congregation express the language of lament. Even those texts that leaned toward lament were often set to catchy tunes in major keys. Since the ongoing tragedies of life cannot be ignored, however, more composers and lyricists are offering song selections to help congregations express words of pain, grief, sorrow, and even anger.

- ### *If not here, then where?*

If our churches are not a safe place to express despair, pain, grief, and anger, then where is a safe place? Since this language is so prevalent in the lives of our congregants, we must offer them a venue to express those emotions or they will look for another place more accepting of that kind of language. Walter Brueggemann suggests that "in a society that is increasingly shut down in terms of public speech, the church in all of its pastoral practices may be the community where the silenced are authorized to voice."³

Bibliography

Albom, Mitch. *The Five People You Meet in Heaven*. New York: Hyperion, 2003.

Berglund, Brad. *Reinventing Sunday: Breakthrough Ideas for Transforming Worship*. Valley Forge: Judson, 2001.

Best, Harold M. "Authentic Worship and Artistic Action." Address to the Calvin Institute of Worship, 2005.

———. *Dumbfounded Praying*. Eugene, OR: Wipf & Stock, 2011.

———. *Unceasing Worship: Biblical Perspectives on Worship and the Arts*. Downers Grove, IL: InterVarsity, 2003.

Borchert, Gerald L. *John 12–21*. The New American Commentary. Nashville: Broadman & Holman, 2002.

Branch, Tara. "It's Not What's Happening, It's How You Respond." *Life*. HuffPost Plus, May 3, 2013. https://www.huffpost.com/entry/acceptance_b_3211053.

Brueggeman, Walter. "The Friday Voice of Faith." *Calvin Theological Journal* 36 (April 2001): 107–13.

———. "Voice as Counter to Violence." *Calvin Theological Journal* 36 (April 2001): 22–33.

Buckingham, Marcus, and Curt Coffman. *First, Break All the Rules: What the World's Greatest Managers Do Differently*. New York: Simon and Shuster, 1999.

Burgess, John. "Why Scripture Matters: Reading the Bible in a Time of Church Conflict." In *A More Profound Alleluia: Theology and Worship in Harmony*, edited by Leanne Van Dyk, 64–69. Grand Rapids: Eerdmans, 2005.

Carson, D. A., ed. *Worship by the Book*. Grand Rapids: Zondervan, 2002.

Carson, Timothy L. "Liminal Reality and Transformational Power: Pastoral Interpretation and Method." *Journal of Pastoral Theology* 7 (Summer 1997): 99.

———. *Transforming Worship*. St. Louis: Chalice, 2003.

Chafin, Kenneth. "Discovering and Preaching the Ordinances Again for the First Time." In *Proclaiming the Baptist Vision: Baptism and the Lord's Supper*, edited by Walter B. Shurden, 129. Macon: Smyth & Helwys, 1999.

Cook, E. T., and Alexander Wedderburn, eds. *The Works of John Ruskin*. New York: Longmans, Green and Co., 1903.

Cordeiro, Wayne. *Leading on Empty: Refilling Your Tank and Renewing Your Passion*. Minneapolis: Bethany House, 2009.

Derber, Charles. *The Pursuit of Attention: Power and Ego in Everyday Life*. Boston: G. K. Hall, 1979.

Dictionary.com. "Awful." Accessed April 21, 2020. https://www.dictionary.com/browse/awful?s=t.

Dillard, Annie. *Teaching a Stone to Talk*. New York: Harper Perennial, 2008.

Ferguson, Everett. "The Lord's Supper in Church History: The Early Church through the Medieval Period." In *The Lord's Supper: Believers Church Perspectives*, edited by Dale R. Stoffer, 21–45. Scottdale: Herald, 1997.

Foster, Richard J. *Celebration of Discipline*. San Francisco: HarperCollins, 1978.

———. *Freedom of Simplicity: Finding Harmony in a Complex World*. New York: HarperOne, 2005.

Frame, John M. *Worship in Spirit and Truth: A Refreshing Study of the Principles and Practice of Biblical Worship*. Phillipsburg: Presbyterian and Reformed, 1996.

Freeman, Martha. "Has God Forsaken Us?" *The Covenant Companion*, November 2001.

Furr, Gary, and Milburn Price. *The Dialogue of Worship: Creating Space for Revelation and Response*. Macon: Smyth & Helwys, 1998.

Gearon, Michael. "Cognitive Biases—The Bandwagon Effect." *Medium*, September 9, 2018. https://medium.com/@michaelgearon/cognitive-biases-social-proof-the-bandwagon-effect-42aa07781fcc.

Grassi, Fr. Dominic. *Bumping into God: Finding Grace in Unexpected Places*. Chicago: Loyola, 1999.

Heath, Chip, and Dan Heath. *Switch: How to Change Things When Change Is Hard*. New York: Broadway, 2010.

Jensen, Robin M. *The Substance of Things Seen: Art, Faith, and the Christian Community*. Grand Rapids: Eerdmans, 2004.

Jinkins, Michael. *In the House of the Lord: Inhabiting the Psalms of Lament*. Collegeville: Liturgical Press, 1998.

Kidd, Reggie M. *With One Voice: Discovering Christ's Song in Our Worship*. Grand Rapids: Baker, 2005.

Kulinski, Fr. Ken. "Kairos-God's Time." *CowPi Journal*, October 9, 2003. http://cowpi.com /journal/2003/10/kairos-gods-time.

Labberton, Mark. *The Dangerous Act of Worship: Living God's Call to Justice*. Downers Grove, IL: InterVarsity, 2007.

Lamm, Kenny. "9 Reasons People Aren't Singing in Worship." *Renewing Worship*, June 11, 2014. https://www.renewingworshipnc.org.

Lawrence, Brother. *The Practice of the Presence of God*. Peabody: Hendrickson, 2004.

Lewis, C. S. *God in the Dock*. Grand Rapids: Eerdmans, 1970.

Liesch, Barry. *People in the Presence of God: Models and Directions for Worship*. Grand Rapids: Zondervan, 1988.

Manner, David W. "Leading Choirs Effectively during Change." *Let's Worship*. Winter 2011– 2012, 32.

———. "Small Church MacGyvers." *Worshipleader: Pursuing the Mission of God in Worship*. July/August 2015, 14–16.

Merton, Thomas. *New Seeds of Contemplation*. New Haven: Abbey of Gethsemani, 1961.

Nouwen, Henri J. M. *With Burning Hearts*. Maryknoll, NY: Orbis, 1994.

Old, Hughes Oliphant. *Leading in Prayer: A Workbook for Worship*. Grand Rapids: Eerdmans, 1995.

Peterson, Eugene H. *Answering God: The Psalms as Tools for Prayer*. San Francisco: Harper, 1989.

———. *Christ Plays in Ten Thousand Places: A Conversation in Spiritual Theology*. Grand Rapids: Eerdmans, 2005.

Redonet, Fernando Lillo. "How Julius Caesar Started a Big War by Crossing a Small Stream." *History Magazine*. National Geographic, March/April, 2017. https://www.national geographic.com/archaeology-and-history/magazine/2017/03-04/julius-caesar -crossing-rubicon-rome/.

Ruis, David. *The Justice God Is Seeking: Responding to the Heart of God through Compassionate Worship*. Ventura, CA: Regal, 2006.

Satterlee, Craig A. *When God Speaks through Change: Preaching in Times of Congregational Transition*. Herndon, VA: Alban Institute, 2005.

Schmit, Clayton J. "Art for Faith's Sake." In *Worship at the Next Level: Insight from Contemporary Views*, edited by Tim A. Dearborn and Scott Coil, 156–62. Eugene: Wipf and Stock, 2004. Chapter originally published Fall 2001 in *Theology, News, and Notes*.

Science Alert Staff. "This Magical Tree Produces 40 Different Types of Fruit." *Science Alert*. June 22, 2018. https://www.sciencealert.com/40-types-of-fruit-tree-artwork-van -aken-2018.

Scott, David. *The Love That Made Mother Teresa*. Manchester, NH: Sophia Institute Press, 2013.

Stanley, Andy. *The Next Generation Leader*. Colorado Springs: Multnomah, 2003.

Stookey, Laurence Hull. *Calendar: Christ's Time for the Church*. Nashville: Abingdon, 1996.

Temple, William. "Temple on the Definition of Worship." *The Institute for Biblical Worship*, December 28, 2016. https://www.biblicalworship.com.

Tersteegan, Gerhard. "Within the Holy Place." *Hymnophile*, May 8, 2008, https://hymno phile.wordpress.com/2008/05/08/within-the-holy-place/.

Tippen, Darryl. *Pilgrim Heart: The Way of Jesus in Everyday Life*. Abilene, TX: Leafwood, 2006.

Tozer, A. W. *The Knowledge of the Holy*. New York: HarperCollins, 1961.

———. *The Pursuit of God*. Vancouver: Eremitical Press, 2009.

The United Methodist Hymnal. Nashville: United Methodist Publishing House, 1991.

Vander Zee, Leonard J. *Christ, Baptism and the Lord's Supper*. Downers Grove, IL: InterVarsity, 2004.

Webber, Robert, ed. *The Services of the Christian Year*. Vol. 5, *The Complete Library of Christian Worship*. Peabody, MA: Hendrickson, 1993.

Webber, Robert E. *Ancient-Future Worship: Proclaiming and Enacting God's Narrative*. Grand Rapids: Baker, 2008.

———. *The Divine Embrace: Recovering the Passionate Spiritual Life*. Grand Rapids: Baker, 2006.

———. *Encountering the Healing Power of God: A Study in the Sacred Actions of Worship*. Peabody, MA: Hendrickson, 1998.

———. *Worship Is a Verb: Celebrating God's Mighty Deeds of Salvation*. 2nd ed. Peabody, MA: Hendrickson, 1996.

Wesley, Charles. "Love Divine All Loves Excelling," *Hymns for Those That Seek, and Those That Have Redemption in the Blood of Jesus Christ*. London, 1747.

Bibliography

Willimon, William H. *Preaching and Leading Worship*. Philadelphia: Westminster, 1984.

Wilson, Marc. "The Psychological Roots of Tall Poppy Syndrome." *New Zealand Listener*, April 3, 2019. https://www.noted.co.nz/health/health-psychology/the-psychological -roots-of-tall-poppy-syndrome.

Witvliet, John D. "A Time to Weep: Liturgical Lament in Times of Crisis." *Reformed Worship* 44 (June 1997): 22–26.

———. *Worship Seeking Understanding: Windows into Christian Practice*. Grand Rapids: Baker, 2003.

Worship Sourcebook, The. Grand Rapids: The Calvin Institute of Christian Worship, Faith Alive Christian Resources, and Baker, 2004.

Yaconelli, Michael. *Dangerous Wonder: The Adventure of Childlike Faith*. Colorado Springs: NavPress, 1998.

York, Terry W., and C. David Bolin. *The Voice of Our Congregation: Seeking and Celebrating God's Song for Us*. Nashville: Abingdon, 2005.

Notes

1. Creating Worship Tourists

1. Annie Dillard, *Teaching a Stone to Talk* (New York: Harper Perennial, 2008), 52.

2. William H. Willimon, *Preaching and Leading Worship* (Philadelphia: Westminster, 1984), 20.

4. Tall Poppy

1. David Manner, "Small Church MacGyvers," *Worshipleader: Pursuing the Mission of God in Worship*, July/August 2015, 14–16. Portions of this chapter first appeared in this magazine article.

2. Marc Wilson, "The Psychological Roots of Tall Poppy Syndrome," *New Zealand Listener*, April 3, 2019, https://www.noted.co.nz/health/health-psychology/the-psychological-roots-of-tall-poppy-syndrome.

6. Tree of 40 Fruit

1. A. W. Tozer, *The Pursuit of God* (Vancouver, BC: Eremitical Press, 2009), 90.

2. Tozer, *The Pursuit of God*, 90.

3. Science Alert Staff, "This Magical Tree Produces 40 Different Types of Fruit," *ScienceAlert*, June 22, 2018, https://www.sciencealert.com/40-types-of-fruit-tree-artwork-van-aken-2018.

8. Bandwagon Effect

1. Adapted from Michael Gearon, "Cognitive Biases—The Bandwagon Effect," *Medium*, September 9, 2018, https://medium.com/@michaelgearon/cognitive-biases -social-proof-the-bandwagon-effect-42aa07781fcc.

10. Falling Up

1. See Appendix 6, "Congregational Suggestions for the Language of Lament."

2. David Scott, *The Love That Made Mother Teresa* (Manchester: Sophia Institute Press, 2013), 107–13.

3. Walter Brueggeman, "The Friday Voice of Faith," *Calvin Theological Journal* 36 (April 2001): 15.

4. Michael Jinkins, *In the House of the Lord: Inhabiting the Psalms of Lament* (Collegeville: Liturgical Press, 1998), 36.

5. Martha Freeman, "Has God Forsaken Us?" *The Covenant Companion* (November 2001): 8.

12. Please, Sir, I Want Some More

1. Kenneth Chafin, "Discovering and Preaching the Ordinances Again for the First Time," in *Proclaiming the Baptist Vision: Baptism and the Lord's Supper*, ed. Walter B. Shurden (Macon: Smyth & Helwys, 1999), 129.

2. See Appendix 2 for a sample of the Lord's Supper questionnaire.

13. Remember

1. Wayne Cordeiro, *Leading on Empty: Refilling Your Tank and Renewing Your Passion* (Minneapolis: Bethany House, 2009), 28.

14. Cause and Effect

1. Richard Foster, *Celebration of Discipline* (San Francisco: HarperCollins, 1978), 158.

2. See Fr. Dominic Grassi, *Bumping into God: Finding Grace in Unexpected Places* (Chicago: Loyola Press, 1999).

16. Loss Leader Easter

1. Laurence Hull Stookey, *Calendar: Christ's Time for the Church* (Nashville: Abingdon, 1996), 53.

2. William M. James, *United Methodist Hymnal* (Nashville: United Methodist Publishing House, 1991).

3. John D. Witvliet, *Worship Seeking Understanding: Windows into Christian Practice* (Grand Rapids: Baker, 2003), 290.

19. Gotta Serve Somebody

1. Mark Labberton, *The Dangerous Act of Worship: Living God's Call to Justice* (Downers Grove, IL: InterVarsity, 2007), 13.

2. Labberton, *The Dangerous Act of Worship*, 71.

3. David Ruis, *The Justice God Is Seeking: Responding to the Heart of God through Compassionate Worship* (Ventura, CA: Regal, 2006), 29.

22. Buyer's Remorse

1. David Manner, "Leading Choirs Effectively during Change," *Let's Worship*, Winter 2011–2012, 32.

2. Andy Stanley, *The Next Generation Leader* (Colorado Springs: Multnomah, 2003), 75.

3. Peter Senge in Brad Berglund, *Reinventing Sunday: Breakthrough Ideas for Transforming Worship* (Valley Forge: Judson, 2001), 11.

4. Chip Heath and Dan Heath, *Switch: How to Change Things When Change Is Hard* (New York: Broadway Books, 2010), 290.

5. Stanley, *The Next Generation Leader*, 50.

6. Stanley, *The Next Generation Leader*, 51.

23. Conversational Narcissists

1. Robert E. Webber, *Ancient-Future Worship: Proclaiming and Enacting God's Narrative* (Grand Rapids: Baker, 2008), 39.

2. Charles Derber, *The Pursuit of Attention: Power and Ego in Everyday Life* (Boston: G. K. Hall, 1979), 26–27.

3. Robert Webber, *The Divine Embrace: Recovering the Passionate Spiritual Life* (Grand Rapids: Baker, 2006), 231.

4. C. S. Lewis, *God in the Dock* (Grand Rapids: Eerdmans, 1970), 212.

5. Harold M. Best, *Unceasing Worship: Biblical Perspectives on Worship and the Arts* (Downers Grove, IL: InterVarsity, 2003), 165–66.

24. Starting a Fire from Scratch

1. D. A. Carson, ed., *Worship by the Book* (Grand Rapids: Zondervan, 2002), 50.

2. Harold M. Best, *Unceasing Worship: Biblical Perspectives on Worship and the Arts* (Downers Grove, IL: InterVarsity, 2003), 9.

25. Is Hallmark Planning Your Services?

1. Timothy L. Carson, *Transforming Worship* (St. Louis: Chalice, 2003), 57.

2. Barry Liesch, *People in the Presence of God: Models and Directions for Worship* (Grand Rapids: Zondervan, 1988), 223.

3. Carson, *Transforming Worship*, 56.

4. Harold M. Best, *Unceasing Worship: Biblical Perspectives on Worship and the Arts* (Downers Grove, IL: InterVarsity, 2003), 17.

5. Best, *Unceasing Worship*, 163.

6. Robert E. Webber, ed., *The Complete Library of Christian Worship*, vol. 5, The Services of the Christian Year (Peabody: Hendrickson, 1993), 82–83.

26. Measure Twice, Cut Once

1. Hughes Oliphant Old, *Leading in Prayer: A Workbook for Worship* (Grand Rapids: Eerdmans, 1995), 5.

2. Harold M. Best, *Dumbfounded Praying* (Eugene: Wipf & Stock, 2011), xii.

3. Old, *Leading in Prayer*, 5.

27. Sing Me into Heaven

1. William Temple, "Temple on the Definition of Worship," The Institute for Biblical Worship, December 28, 2016, http://biblicalworship.com/wqotw/2016/12/28/temple-on-the-definition-of-worship.

2. Darryl Tippen, *Pilgrim Heart: The Way of Jesus in Everyday Life* (Abilene: Leafwood, 2006), 148.

3. Reggie M. Kidd, *With One Voice: Discovering Christ's Song in Our Worship* (Grand Rapids: Baker, 2005), 14.

4. Tippen, *Pilgrim Heart*, 150.

28. Scriptureless

1. Robert E. Webber, *Ancient-Future Worship: Proclaiming and Enacting God's Narrative* (Grand Rapids: Baker, 2008), 113.

2. John M. Frame, *Worship in Spirit and Truth: A Refreshing Study of the Principles and Practice of Biblical Worship* (Phillipsburg: Presbyterian and Reformed, 1996), 90.

3. Webber, *Ancient-Future Worship*, 113–14.

4. Webber, *Ancient-Future Worship*, 130.

5. John Burgess, "Why Scripture Matters: Reading the Bible in a Time of Church Conflict," in *A More Profound Alleluia: Theology and Worship in Harmony*, ed. Leanne Van Dyk (Grand Rapids: Eerdmans, 2005), 66.

30. Getting Rid of Volunteers

1. Marcus Buckingham and Curt Coffman, *First, Break All the Rules: What the World's Greatest Managers Do Differently* (New York: Simon and Shuster, 1999), 11–13.

2. See Appendix 4 for a worship leader and worship team relational contract sample.

3. Buckingham and Coffman, *First, Break All the Rules*, 11–13.

31. Jump in the Deep End

1. Clayton J. Schmit, "Art for Faith's Sake," in *Worship at the Next Level: Insight from Contemporary Voices*, ed. Tim A. Dearborn and Scott Coil (Eugene: Wipf and Stock, 2004), 157.

2. Robin M. Jensen, *The Substance of Things Seen: Art, Faith, and the Christian Community* (Grand Rapids: Eerdmans, 2004), 2.

3. Robert E. Webber, *Worship Is a Verb: Celebrating God's Mighty Deeds of Salvation*, 2nd ed. (Peabody: Hendrickson, 1996), 183.

4. Harold M. Best, "Authentic Worship and Artistic Action," address to the Calvin Institute of Worship, 2005.

32. Building a Wall

1. Chip Heath and Dan Heath, *Switch: How to Change Things When Change Is Hard* (New York: Broadway Books, 2010), 55.

2. Craig A. Satterlee, *When God Speaks through Change: Preaching in Times of Congregational Transition* (Herndon: Alban Institute, 2005), 6.

33. Not Our Kind of People

1. Harold Best, *Unceasing Worship: Biblical Perspectives on Worship and the Arts* (Downers Grove, IL: InterVarsity, 2003), 181.

2. Mitch Albom, *The Five People You Meet in Heaven* (New York: Hyperion, 2003), 94.

3. Best, *Unceasing Worship*, 181.

34. False Dichotomy

1. Kenny Lamm, "9 Reasons People Aren't Singing in Worship," *Renewing Worship*, June 11, 2014, https://www.renewingworshipnc.org.

35. Secret Worshipper

1. See Appendix 3 for a secret worshipper questionnaire.

36. Play the Ball Where the Monkey Drops It

1. Thomas Merton, *New Seeds of Contemplation* (New Haven: Abbey of Gethsemani, 1961), 58.

2. Tara Branch, "It's Not What's Happening, It's How You Respond," *Life*. HuffPost Plus, May 3, 2013, https://www.huffpost.com/entry/acceptance_b_3211053.

37. Wasting Time

1. Fr. Ken Kulinski, "Kairos-God's Time," *CowPi Journal*, October 9, 2003, http://cowpi.com/journal/2003/10/kairos-gods-time.

38. Cheap Worship

1. Terry W. York and C. David Bolin, *The Voice of Our Congregation: Seeking and Celebrating God's Song for Us* (Nashville: Abingdon, 2005), 112.

39. We're Talking about Practice

1. Brother Lawrence, *The Practice of the Presence of God* (Peabody: Hendrickson, 2004), 97.

2. Lawrence, *The Practice of the Presence of God*, 42.

3. Lawrence, *The Practice of the Presence of God*, xii.

4. Lawrence, *The Practice of the Presence of God*, 18.

5. Harold Best, *Unceasing Worship: Biblical Perspectives on Worship and the Arts* (Downers Grove, IL: InterVarsity, 2003), 99.

40. Worship Karaoke

1. Terry W. York and C. David Bolin, *The Voice of Our Congregation: Seeking and Celebrating God's Song for Us* (Nashville: Abingdon, 2005), 9.

2. York and Bolin, *Voice of Our Congregation*, 9.

41. Stop Singing

1. Gary A. Furr and Milburn Price, *The Dialogue of Worship: Creating Space for Revelation and Response* (Macon: Smyth & Helwys, 1998), 90.

2. E. T. Cook and Alexander Wedderburn, eds., *The Works of John Ruskin* (New York: Longmans, Green and Co., 1903), 247.

3. Richard J. Foster, *Freedom of Simplicity: Finding Harmony in a Complex World* (New York: HarperOne, 2005), 68.

42. Awful Worship

1. "Awful," Dictionary.com, accessed April 21, 2020, https://www.dictionary.com/browse/awful?s=t

2. Michael Yaconelli, *Dangerous Wonder: The Adventure of Childlike Faith* (Colorado Springs: NavPress, 1998), 28.

3. A. W. Tozer, *The Knowledge of the Holy* (New York: HarperCollins, 1961), 18.

4. Gerald L. Borchert, *John 12–21*, The New American Commentary (Nashville: Broadman & Holman, 2002), 104.

5. Yaconelli, *Dangerous Wonder*, 23.

6. Yaconelli, *Dangerous Wonder*, 24.

7. Robert E. Webber, *The Divine Embrace: Recovering the Passionate Spiritual Life* (Grand Rapids: Baker, 2006), 87.

8. Charles Wesley, "Love Divine All Loves Excelling," *Hymns for Those That Seek, and Those That Have Redemption in the Blood of Jesus Christ* (London, 1747).

44. Crossing the Rubicon

1. Fernando Lillo Redonet, "How Julius Caesar Started a Big War by Crossing a Small Stream," *History Magazine*, National Geographic, March/April 2017, https://www.nationalgeographic.com/archaeology-and-history/magazine/2017/03-04/julius-caesar-crossing-rubicon-rome/.

2. Terry W. York and C. David Bolin, *The Voice of Our Congregation: Seeking and Celebrating God's Song for Us* (Nashville: Abingdon, 2005), 39.

45. Missing the In-Between

1. Arnold van Gennep, *The Rites of Passage* (London: Routledge and Kegan Paul, 1960), referenced in Timothy L. Carson, "Liminal Reality and Transformational Power: Pastoral Interpretation and Method," *Journal of Pastoral Theology* 7 (Summer 1997): 99.

2. Carson, "Liminal Reality and Transformational Power," 100.

3. Carson, "Liminal Reality and Transformational Power," 100.

4. Timothy L. Carson, *Transforming Worship* (St. Louis: Chalice, 2003), 60.

5. Victor Turner, *The Ritual Process: Structure and Anti-Structure* (New York: Aldine, 1969), as referenced in Carson, "Liminal Reality and Transformational Power," 101.

6. Carson, "Liminal Reality and Transformational Power," 101.

47. Send in a Canary

1. Kenny Lamm, "9 Reasons People Aren't Singing in Worship," *Renewing Worship*, June 11, 2014, https://www.renewingworshipnc.org.

2. Lamm, "9 Reasons People Aren't Singing in Worship."

49. More Than a Memorial

1. Everett Ferguson, "The Lord's Supper in Church History: The Early Church through the Medieval Period," in *The Lord's Supper: Believers Church Perspectives*, ed. Dale R. Stoffer (Scottdale: Herald, 1997), 22.

2. Leonard J. Vander Zee, *Christ, Baptism and the Lord's Supper* (Downers Grove, IL: InterVarsity, 2004), 157.

3. Henri J. M. Nouwen, *With Burning Hearts* (Maryknoll, NY: Orbis, 1994), 95–96.

4. Nouwen, *With Burning Hearts*, 96.

5. Robert E. Webber, *Encountering the Healing Power of God: A Study in the Sacred Actions of Worship* (Peabody, MA: Hendrickson, 1998), 27.

Conclusion

1. Eugene H. Peterson, *Christ Plays in Ten Thousand Places: A Conversation in Spiritual Theology* (Grand Rapids: Eerdmans, 2005), 71.

Appendix 1: Worship Evaluation Questionnaire

1. *The Worship Sourcebook* (Grand Rapids: The Calvin Institute of Christian Worship, Faith Alive Christian Resources, and Baker, 2004), 763.

Appendix 6: Congregational Suggestions for the Language of Lament

1. John D. Witvliet, "A Time to Weep: Liturgical Lament in Times of Crisis," *Reformed Worship* 44 (June 1997): 22.

2. Eugene Peterson, *Answering God: The Psalms as Tools for Prayer* (San Francisco: Harper, 1989), 3.

3. Walter Brueggemann, "Voice as Counter to Violence," *Calvin Theological Journal* 36 (April 2001): 25.

CPSIA information can be obtained
at www.ICGtesting.com
Printed in the USA
BVHW071530160321
602607BV00002B/10